Global Revolutionary Terrorism

Global Revolutionary Terrorism

THE FORGOTTEN THREAT OF RUSSIA'S
CLANDESTINE WAR AGAINST THE
UNITED STATES OF AMERICA

• • •

Lance Alred

ISBN: 1532841663
ISBN 13: 9781532841668
Library of Congress Control Number: 2016908303
CreateSpace Independent Publishing Platform
North Charleston, South Carolina

Contents

Author's Note ·ix
Prologue· xvii
Introduction ·xxi

Chapter 1 The Modern Russian System of State Security · · · · · · · · · · · 1
Chapter 2 The Soviet Exploitation of Islam and Muslims · · · · · · · · · · · 8
Chapter 3 A Brief Word on the Iranian Special Services · · · · · · · · · · · 13
Chapter 4 The Foundation of Putin's Russia· · · · · · · · · · · · · · · · · · 18
Chapter 5 Cold/Insurrectional Warfare · 38
Chapter 6 Dr. Ezepchuk on the Cheka · 48

Conclusion/Investigative Summary· · · · · · · · · · · · · · · · · · · 61
Bibliography· 71
Appendix 1· 73
Appendix 2: Suggested Further Reading and Viewing · · · · 77
About the Author· 79

Do not let anyone claim tribute of American patriotism if they even attempt to remove religion from politics.
—George Washington, "Farewell Address to the Nation"

Gentlemen, comrades, do not be concerned about all you hear about Glasnost and Perestroika and democracy in the coming years. They are primarily for outward consumption. There will be no significant internal changes in the Soviet Union, other than for cosmetic purposes. Our purpose is to disarm the Americans and let them fall asleep.
—Mikhail Gorbachev, November 1987

Author's Note

• • •

Unless otherwise noted, this book is a personal narrative based on notes I took during interviews, lectures, personal experiences, and discussions with professors while earning my MA in Russian, along with meetings with one of my sources, Dr. Yuri Ezepchuk, and an acquaintance from a leading research university in Moscow. Although names are not included for safety and security reasons in most cases, Dr. Ezepchuk did express his desire to be cited in this book.

Dr. Ezepchuk worked under the experimental-sciences program of the Union of Soviet Socialist Republics (USSR); this program was the foundation for the creation of weapons of mass destruction (WMDs) under the direct supervision of the KGB and the Soviet Ministry of Defense. Dr. Ezepchuk was an anthrax expert who worked on bacteriological weapons projects and developed vaccines against anthrax. He then became a research scientist for Russia's progressive Gamaleya Research Institute of Epidemiology and Microbiology, where he founded the Laboratory of Molecular Bases of Bacterial Pathogenicity, specializing in modeling the enzymes, toxins, and antigens produced by a variety of pathogens. He developed the biological concept of the "bacterial pathogenicity phenomenon," which he outlined in two academic publications and dissertations. Dr. Ezepchuk holds a PhD in biochemistry, a doctorate of biological sciences, and the title of professor; in 1993, he was subsequently invited by the US government to conduct research at the National Jewish Medical Research Center and the Biomedical Center of the University of Colorado.

Since 2003 I have been very fortunate and blessed to have had numerous opportunities to conduct extensive research in the fields of Russian language and related area studies (as well as training in Russian martial arts), both here in the United States and in Russia. Because the overwhelming majority of this book is based on personal experience, interviews, and discussion notes that I took during my Russian-language MA studies, I would like to provide the reader with a very brief overview of my experiences related to the former Soviet Union.

In March of 2004, I began to teach myself Russian on a regular and consistent basis. From June to October 2004, I took my first formal Russian language courses, first at Arapahoe Community College and then at the Berlitz Language Schools. At Berlitz, my instructor was the aforementioned Dr. Ezepchuk; he was an excellent teacher of the Russian language and was a major reason I gained proficiency so quickly. Dr. Ezepchuk, a colleague of Ken Alibek (coauthor of the book *Biohazard*) and close acquaintance of Andrei Sakharov (the famous Soviet nuclear physicist who developed the Soviet hydrogen bomb and later dissident), worked under top-secret KGB scientific-military programs.

In January 2005, after the police department I worked for kindly allowed me to go to part-time status to pursue intensive academic and professional education and training, I began studies for a BA in global studies and Russian language at the University of Denver. Under the direction of the Russian professors there, my proficiency in Russian continued to improve. I was able to achieve the necessary level of Russian proficiency required to participate in and complete study-abroad programs in Russia through a partnering international organization.

My most recent study-abroad period was part of my MA in Russian, which included an academic year (September 2012 to May 2013) spent in Moscow. I lived in a Soviet-style apartment in the center of Moscow, a twenty-five-minute walk from the Kremlin and Red Square. From the apartment, I could see the upper section of the castle-like Ministry of Foreign Affairs building, the upper portion of the American Embassy, the Russian White House (a government administration building that came under attack during the 1993 coup attempt), and the Hotel Ukraine.

During this extremely enriching program, I completed the required graduate-degree coursework in several subjects, including linguistics and Russian cultural history, politics, and literature. I completed coursework at two major universities in Moscow.[1] At one of these, I took a course on American history and government in which I was the only American. This course, as with all other courses I took in Russia, was conducted entirely in Russian, among Russian students. I enrolled in the course because I wanted to gain insight into how Russians perceive Americans and their history and to find out exactly what Russians are taught about the United States. An overwhelming amount of material was extremely leftist in nature, including the works of Howard Zinn, and we spent a great deal of time on how the rich, white, ruling elite and Freemasons exploit the population to maximize profit and maintain complete power and control over the masses—especially poor whites, blacks, Latinos, and American Indians. The works of Zinn, especially *A People's History of the United States*, were mandatory reading for students desiring careers in politics, economics, and the special services; they provided a solid theoretical basis for continuing the race conflict in the United States. The race aspect is one angle of attack in facilitating class warfare and insurrection, which are two crucial elements of Marxism-Leninism.

At the other university, I completed coursework in the field of international security. The instructor was a retired major general in the Soviet/Russian army and a professor at a Russian think tank that is highly influential in "assisting" American experts on Russia in Russian foreign and domestic policy.

While working in Central Asia for an international organization, I had a very unique homestay in Almaty, Kazakhstan. The Kazakh host mother (whom I will call "ZA") was a Muslim convert to Protestantism.

---

1 I cannot provide the names of the schools (or of the professors and students I interviewed there) due to security risks for both them and myself, since these schools are where high-ranking Russian military and government officials and their relatives work and study.

I was amazed at how much she knew about the Bible and how she applied Christian principles to all aspects of her life. When her husband passed away, praying five times a day at the mosque did not heal her pain, even after five years. Fortunately, through her daughter's work, ZA became acquainted with an ob-gyn doctor with whom her daughter worked who was also a Muslim convert to Protestantism. This doctor insisted that the only way to heal was through God. ZA began to study the Bible with her and prayed constantly. Eventually, she was able to get over her pain; with other problems that arise to this day, she always looks to God despite the Kazakh and Russian governments' mission to discredit Western Christianity globally.

The main points ZA conveyed during our last conversation before I left Kazakhstan because of a life-threatening emergency situation may be summarized as follows:

1) We need to do and say nothing but good things for and about others. Ask people how they are doing and listen to them with empathy. If you are in a position to do so, help the other person in any way you can. Always try to help people feel good about themselves.
2) Without God you will go nowhere and will not be able to experience true happiness and joy on earth.
3) Give more than you get.
4) Only in quiet moments of contemplation can you truly hear God's gentle voice. If one listens attentively, God's voice sends a person on the road to happiness; troubles and problems will occur for everyone, though, regardless of how "good" a person is. Looking to Jesus Christ of Nazareth puts everything in life into proper perspective.
5) Sometimes God communicates to you through other people and events.
6) Don't dwell on the problem at hand; focus only on God, joy, and love. A few times every day, starting first thing in the morning, thank God and truly feel grateful and appreciative for your health,

vision, hearing, ability to walk and taste, the people in your life, and the experiences you've had—both good and bad.

7) Don't forget about God in your daily routines. Remember, things happen only through God.

8) ZA could not find peace in Islam.[2] Bear her experience in mind and remember that only Jesus Christ of Nazareth can give peace and help people. We need to pray constantly, even when things are good. Bad things happen so that we have no choice but to turn to God and improve our relationship with Him.

9) Don't ask God for specific material things; only ask for His help and guidance to stay on track, do His will, and to be with Him and close to Him. In order to do this, she said, I must find a good church and go as often as possible, because good things cannot happen without God's involvement.

I do my best to follow ZA's advice to this day. It is easy to drift away, but Christians need to do our best in this area. Americans' connections to God is the only thing that will save our great nation. It is interesting to note that ZA said that Muhammad was instructed by Allah that if Muslims are in great trouble and/or danger, they need to look to the Christians.

More recently in the United States, working as an armed transit security officer for the Regional Transportation District (RTD) in Denver, I had a front-row seat to a concept known as "criminal radicalism" there. Criminal radicalism is a form of revolutionary terrorism/insurrectional warfare. I talked to gang members who admitted to me that they were acting as agitators by protesting fare prices throughout Denver and the surrounding area under the direction of a political organization based in Chicago. Unfortunately, everyone I have talked to has refused to disclose the name of this entity. In talking to various known gang members

---

2 ZA informed me that Islam is not a true religion because Muhammad was a false prophet. Therefore, Islam is essentially a political ideology with a moral code and some religious connotations. ZA further explained to me that Islamic sectarian violence occurs rarely. The majority of struggles between sects are actually based on territory and/or political influence rather than interpretation of the Koran.

(identified by the Denver Police Department), I was informed that the harsh economic conditions (related to the high costs of living from the lack of adequate employment opportunities for the masses) have caused people to resort to crime in order to get by. At the same time, their illicit activities provide ample unhindered sources of income while simultaneously creating chaos in society.

Since the City and County of Denver judicial system is so overloaded, these gang members encounter no difficulties in overtly gambling and selling drugs on RTD property—on camera—because they know that nothing will happen to them. The gang members and drug dealers make sales to boys and girls and men and women of all races and socioeconomic backgrounds, including businesspeople in suits and ties. And with the legalization of marijuana in Colorado, many drug-related cases have overwhelmed the system. Gang members and the people who call the shots, "shot callers," appear to have given a green light to create chaos and disorder by harassing, intimidating, and assaulting RTD drivers and staff members. The situation has deteriorated to the extent that the Black Panther Party is working closely with the Crips gang in Denver. I also identified an agent of Russia's Federal Service for Control of Drug Trafficking (FSKN) as being in charge of the major drug dealers whom the Denver Police Department has identified on Civic Center Station property. The FSKN plays a major role in supporting Russian organized crime in the United States.

The FSKN was known as the Committee of State Control of Trafficking of Drugs and Psychotropic Substances until March of 2004. In addition to drug trafficking and enforcement operations, both domestically (i.e., in Russia) and internationally, this agency also has propaganda and psyops (psychological operations) responsibilities. The FSKN operates the magazine *NARKOMAT,* which is an abbreviation for the People's Commissariat, whose motto (as of 2016) is "For the USSR!" This agency's magazine promotes the international communist movement. The corresponding journal is *Anti-Dose,* a youth magazine for the proletariat revolution that promotes family values, nonviolence, peace, and so on.

Another disturbing discovery I made while working at Civic Center Station was the connection of what are known as the "Juggalos" to what is known as the Fuck the Police protest movement, which in turn is connected to the communism-inspired Occupy movement in Denver. The Juggalos are a gang (fans of the horrorcore rap group the Insane Clown Posse) that has been known to commit acts of violence by the use of swords, machetes, and hatchets; gang members are known for wearing black-and-white clown face paint. In late May and early June of 2016, the Denver police and RTD transit security officers dealt with Juggalos who were protesting against law enforcement in Denver's popular Sixteenth Street mall area. Interestingly, one of the rappers from the Insane Clown Posse has familial connections to a wrestler known as the Great Milenko, who was originally from Moscow. In addition to being involved in various types of serious crimes, law enforcement believes that the Juggalos are also active in domestic terrorism.

The final item of significance from my work at Civic Center Station is people wearing the red Soviet star with Lenin's head on their jackets and shirts. Given the fact that the Black Panthers and Malcolm X identified with Marxism-Leninism, this revival of the ideology demands further investigation into the role of agents and officers of the Russian special services in fomenting revolution in Denver, including the FSKN operative I encountered.

Another transit security officer I worked with at the Civic Center is an expert on gangs; he said that he had observed someone with a Pakistani Special Forces armband and an individual with an MS-13 (for the transnational criminal organization "Mara Salvatrucha") tattoo on the back of his head hanging out with gang members. Pakistani Special Forces are close partners with the Iranian Quds Force, the latter of which will be briefly discussed later in this book.

Prologue

• • •

IT SEEMS THAT ALL WE hear about in the news is how awful things are in the world today. The media bombards us with the threat ISIS/IS poses to the world, the Syrian War, the Ukraine crisis, China's aggressive economic actions (and how it is buying the most expensive real estate in the United States while working with Russia to destroy and replace the dollar), cyberattacks by Russia and China against the United States, North Korean missile launches, and so on. Regarding ISIS, dozens of experts are called upon to provide an analysis of how a terrorist organization such as ISIS can be dealt with, particularly in the wake of the latest terrorist attack. Unfortunately, none of the diplomatic or military solutions they propose are viable, because the root causes of international terrorism are not fully comprehended thanks to the effective operations of foreign nations' agents of influence in conjunction with information-warfare operations, particularly involving those individuals who work in or with think tanks that help Americans "interpret" global dynamics.

It is important to note that Palestinian Liberation Organization (PLO) militants, Al-Qaeda and its affiliates, and now ISIS/IS had (and continue to have) the primary goal of maintaining the constant global condition of revolution by dragging out the necessity for military action—also the goal of the ongoing communist/Russian revolution to drain the natural, economic, and human resources of the West. Victory is not the immediate goal. Ultimately, the state of revolution must be maintained as the world transitions to global socialism on the way to constructing global communism and global governance through a plethora of organizations. This process is both an art and a science and is constantly evolving. Even if ISIS is completely eliminated, a new group will replace it unless the root causes of terrorism are comprehended and addressed.

The name "Islamic State" has been used periodically for centuries to represent and promote Islamic global expansionism and imperialism.[3] Muslims indirectly impose on other faiths the public acceptance of Islamic customs and traditions in the countries to which they migrate. At the moment, the special services (intelligence and security services) of Russia and Iran are using ISIS/IS to signify the rebirth, revival, and expansion of Islam throughout the world. For anyone knowledgeable about Islamic history, this type of symbolism is clear. Americans must also understand that no major terrorist organization can function without the assistance of special services. In addition to violence, the global Islamic renaissance is much more dangerous than was the case earlier in world history because it applies the cunning and manipulative so-called peaceful and humanitarian position of promoting cultural diversity, religious tolerance, and coexistence via the Gülen movement led by the Turkish scholar and cleric Fethullah Gülen.

It is absolutely essential to understand that the Islamic terrorism that is directed against the West today is rooted in the advent of the Marxist-Leninist PLO and the Iranian Revolution of 1979, which itself was rooted in the Russian Revolution of 1917. Both of these global revolutions are currently in full swing. This revolutionary mutation has gained momentum thanks to Lenin and the Communist Party and has been facilitated

---

3 Shortly after the demise of the Soviet Union, retired Soviet Air Force Major General Dzhokhar Dudayev created an experimental "Islamic State" after his colleague Zemlikhan Yandarbiyev (Chairman of the Soviet Writers Union specializing in propaganda) created the necessary socio-political conditions for a separatist movement in conjunction with Movladi Udugov (Head of The Caucasus Emirate News Agency and political figure), Aslan Maskhadov (commander of missile forces in Vilnius, Lithuania whose soldiers provided cover for the capture of the Vilnius television center in 1991), and Shamil Basayev (who participated in the defense of the Russian White House during the 1991 coup). To this day, the Chechen Republic remains an important component of the Russian Federation.

by the Cheka (Russia's political and secret police) and its global partners since Lenin. Again, in conjunction with the violence and chaos associated with the communist world, the strive to maintain the condition of constant revolution is the highly deceptive peaceful approach. This approach includes promoting issues and concepts such as cultural diversity, social-justice movements, religious tolerance, the environment, racism, antipolice protests, and the like. These are all socialist-revolutionary concepts rooted in Marxism-Leninism; they are designed to maintain the state of revolution for the progress of humanity and society alike and are meant to overthrow capitalism. In Marxism-Leninism, various forms of revolution—including armed, cultural, moral, insurrectional, and so on—are necessary elements for society to develop and progress. This concept is a central theme of the Hegelian dialectic, in which there is one position on an issue and an opposing position, then both sides either battle it out or have to engage in dialogue and work together in order to come to a compromise that will then result in a peaceful solution and the unification of culturally diverse masses.

In order to achieve the overarching goal of this book, I argue that there are various forms of global revolutionary terrorism/insurrectional warfare that the United States must contend with. These diverse forms of warfare are designed to bolster violent terrorist attacks with humanitarian strategies and tactics. These elements are necessary in order to understand both the Cold War and Russian leader Vladimir Putin's junta. Contrary to popular opinion, the Cold War is not over. It merely evolved into a more progressive and subtle state in which enemies of America live among us while continuing to infiltrate, influence, and control more and more aspects of American society. The continuation of this process has been gradual (and seemingly unnoticeable) since the dissolution of the USSR but is having catastrophic consequences. The constant and totalitarian challenge of revolutionary warfare is to take the enemy nation captive—not physically but rather psychologically—by altering the enemy's (America's) idcological positions and crushing the spirit of its population. The end result is a state of confusion in which the majority of Americans do not know who our true enemies are or that they are living side by side among us.

Many aspects of American society have been infiltrated by (and are increasingly under the control of) communists from the former Soviet Union and the Warsaw Pact nations, the Muslim world, and elsewhere in Asia, right in front of our eyes. Since communism supposedly collapsed, communists have been operating under the auspices of other labels, including *liberals*, *leftists*, *democrats*, and *social democrats*. Of course, despite the fact that America declared communism a failure in 1991, a communist country, China, holds the majority of our debt.

Many Americans agree that our nation is not what it used to be and often express dissatisfaction with how American society is falling apart. We all know that something is wrong but do not necessarily understand the root causes of why things are the way they are today in this country. The so-called collapse of communism and the dissolution of the Soviet Union was the catalyst of a process that continues to this day. A few of the aspects of society that have been infiltrated and are under attack include the American education system (from elementary school through college), the media, traditional American culture, Western Christianity, certain aspects of big business and the banking industry, the government including the FBI, the CIA, the State Department, the Department of Homeland Security, and the Department of Defense (by employing heritage and native speakers of languages that are critical to US national security, especially Russian, Arabic, Chinese, and Farsi), and, perhaps above all, the American conscience and psyche. The multitiered attack America is currently experiencing is on a scale unprecedented in world history.

Introduction

• • •

The following comes from discussions and lecture notes I took while pursuing my MA in Russian (2012–2013).

THE CENTRAL THESIS OF THIS book is centered upon the various forms of global revolutionary terrorism/insurrection warfare, the role of the Russian special services in facilitating this devastating strategy against the American people and our society, and, of course, Putin's Russia. One of the reasons the United States has been unable to formulate an effective policy on Russia and its allies is due to a lack of understanding of the many nations and the over one-hundred ethnicities that comprised the former Soviet Union and its allies during this period. The problematic school of thought that the Cold War has ended has exacerbated the situation. At the height of the Cold War, US policy toward the Soviets was fairly straightforward; it consisted primarily of responding to specific threats, maintaining a "bipolar" balance of global stability (albeit a fragile one), and advancing military equipment and capabilities. The dimensions of battle in modern warfare have changed significantly since the early 1990s, however, which was a time when the United States was more or less at a loss about what to do about being the alleged winner of the Cold War. This misconception and its associated confusion have led to difficulties in defining the goals of US national security both at home and abroad. Of course, the reality is that American political interests globally are a struggle for strategic spheres of influence that are in opposition to Russia's in the continuation of what is known as the "Great Game."

The Great Game is no longer limited to Central Asia but rather is global in nature. Our traditional approaches to combating threats are increasingly outdated. This book attempts to outline a foundation for the reformation of US foreign policy toward not only Russia and the post-Soviet space but also the entire Eurasian continent and, subsequently, international terrorism (or, more accurately, global revolutionary terrorism). Lenin would be proud that his international revolution is evolving on a global scale, one country at a time, regardless of cultural or religious affiliation/orientation. In fact, Marxism-Leninism is becoming the new norm in the United States. Americans are actively promoting Marxism-Leninism without even realizing it. This book merely presents a brief overview of the dynamics that our nation faces; it is up to each individual reader to further explore any personal topics of interest presented in this text. The appendix may be used as a starting point. Before formulating effective policies toward the Russian threat, we must first educate ourselves about Russia's fascinating cultural history, the Russian system of state security, and the various forms of global revolutionary terrorism, which extend beyond terrorist attacks such as bombings and mass shootings.

• • •

For most of its existence, the Russian Empire primarily relied on farming and associated industries. The conditions in which the average Russian lived were dangerous and difficult; in addition to being under constant attack, their society was also prone to widespread criminal activity. A collective mentality was and continues to be necessary for survival as a result. During the time of the Russian Empire (1721–1917), the ruling elites were highly educated and enlightened, while the rest of the population, who generally lived miserable existences, were lucky if they could read and write. The process of transforming the Russian Empire into the world's first socialist nation—one with a 99 percent literacy rate; a nation that invented television and was the first to put a human in space (for quite some time now, the United States has been using Russian rocket engines for its space program)—was achieved through the revolutionary ideology of the Russian intelligentsia and social democrats globally. These groups of intellectuals have forged, influenced, and shaped the development of global society for the last century in conjunction with the Cheka (the Russian political police). In addition to the armed and violent insurrection facilitated by Russian terrorist organizations, the unification of workers, peasants, and the intelligentsia helped to oust one of the most powerful autocracies in world history and replace it with an even more powerful totalitarian state.

Ever since the French Revolution and the advent of the *Communist Manifesto* (1848) by Karl Marx and Friedrich Engels, revolutionary schools of thought have been advanced on a global scale through both peaceful and violent means. Revolutionary ideology from Western Europe spread to Russia through the connection of the Russian intelligentsia with the elite circles of European society. The Russian intelligentsia began to debate the potential future courses of development of the Russian Empire in order to create a society where the people could thrive. In order to achieve the necessary dynamic transformation within the Russian Empire, the process of radicalization began involving farmers, peasants, the working class, and students under the direction of the intelligentsia.

Russian literary critics, writers, artists, and poets played a crucial role in the dissemination and popularization of opposition (anti-imperialist) ideas; examples include Ilya Repin, Fyodor Tyutchev, Mikhail Bakunin, Alexander Herzen, Ivan Turgenev, Fyodor Dostoyevsky, Leo Tolstoy, Nikolay Nekrasov, Vissarion Belinsky, Nikolay Chernyshevsky, and many others. Russian literature began to reveal major flaws in Russian society through inspirational fictional stories based on actual events. Students and young adults became enlightened and felt that it was up to them to lead the transformation of the Russian Empire into a socialist nation-state. Since the majority of the population were peasants and uneducated laborers, teaching the people how to read and analyze philosophic ideals rooted in socialism and educational reforms was a crucial aspect of this transformation. Significant reforms in Russia did not really begin to occur until the 1860s and 1870s, beginning with the relatively peaceful emancipation of the serfs. At the same time, the ruling elite relied on deceptive tactics and increased the use of violent police actions to maintain control and their political legitimacy.

Russian theorists' initial revolutionary approaches centered on educating and developing people so that they would be able to contribute to future societal development while being able to enjoy the cultural and economic advances of society. At the same time, other theorists called for violent armed insurrection along with a unification of the masses that would culminate in the introduction of socialism by force. It is important to point out that revolutions in Latin America, China, and Iran were also spurred on by students and the intelligentsia. Students and the intelligentsia are the main engines in the process of proliferating revolutionary ideology among the masses, since the average uneducated worker does not necessarily possess these deep philosophical and theoretical tendencies. The poor and uneducated are used as tools for advancing revolutionary objectives through social movements, violence, and armed insurrection.

Therefore, the current war on terror should begin by investigating the potential threats in American educational structures as well as its political, economic, and cultural institutions.

As social movements and violent uprising continued to rise in Russia during this period, secret underground organizations began to form; some mutated into terrorist organizations.[4] An example was the organization known as Land and Freedom, which eventually evolved into the People's Organization. The means these groups used to achieve their goals included propaganda, agitation among the peasantry and other classes of society, and acts of terror against any unsuitable government officials or political police. In fact, this organization was the first to introduce to the world the

---

4 In my opinion, US leaders need to start paying closer attention to the diverse range of social movements and protests that are on the rise in this country, since these types of activities are what led to the Russian Revolution of 1917.

use of bombings as a terrorism tactic. Therefore, one could reasonably say that modern terrorism originated in Russia in the late 1800s.

One part of the People's Organization was eventually transformed into the People's Will, which converted its theoretical basis to Marxism and eventually declared revolutionary terrorism/insurrectional warfare as the primary method of the struggle against capitalism and its exploitation of the masses. The People's Will conducted political assassinations of various members of the tsarist regime, including Tsar Alexander II, as well as bombings of strategic assets.

The assassination of Tsar Alexander II on March 1, 1881, led to the proliferation of revolutionary ideology and the adoption of populism as a secondary tactic to support terrorist operations.[5] Despite the utilization of terrorism as a tactic to overthrow capitalism and maintain the state of revolution, Russian intelligentsia remained the vanguard for achieving socialism by any means necessary. By the mid- to late 1880s, the proliferation of Marxism was transferred to the workers, who would later become the tools of the intelligentsia in maintaining the constant state of revolution as the means of transforming Russia into a socialist society. Eventually, the peasants joined the struggle as well once they became fully radicalized. Essentially, the Soviet Union's strategic reorganization in 1991 into the Commonwealth of Independent States (CIS), an international organization, may actually signify the USSR's transition from socialism to communism. It is also important to note that during the Soviet era, each of the fifteen republics was already "independent," as were the autonomous regions.

With the advent of the industrialization of Russian society, the Marxists confronted the Russian Empire with a new modus operandi: the strikes and protests of workers, who demanded better working conditions, which included everything from worker's compensation to better pay, medical and dental care, and an eight-hour work day, and so on. For

---

5   This combination exists to this day. Both components are essential to maintaining the condition of revolution that is necessary for the capitalist transition to socialism and communism.

the most part, these strikes and protests were conducted peacefully; they eventually became violent, however, when employers refused to negotiate, let alone make any type of concessions. Violent protests and movements were met in kind by Russia's political and secret police. Instigators were identified through the numerous agents who had infiltrated social and terrorist groups.

Eventually, the goal of the intelligentsia's solidarity with workers and peasants in Russia led to national liberation under the guidance and direction of the Cheka. These movements reached their apogee in the Russian Revolution of 1917. The tsarist regime was overthrown and the tsar and his family were murdered, leading to the establishment of a new democratic republic—the Soviet Union. For the majority of the twentieth century, revolutionary national-liberation movements were facilitated globally, led and inspired by Russian revolutionaries and the political police: a process that continues to this day despite the alleged end of communism.

At the heart of this struggle is the Marxist-Leninist perspective of different forms of class struggle and the socioeconomic and cultural oppression of the masses by small groups of the wealthy. Today, Marxism-Leninism has not disappeared but, through the use of deceptive strategies and tactics, has gained expansive momentum under different titles, forms, and organizations. Some organizations have even kept the same names, one example of which is the World Peace Council.[6] More recent manifestations include the international and Islamic terrorism and social movements that advocate for human rights, fair wages, and so on. Today's rhetoric on the themes mentioned above is identical to Marxism-Leninism under different titles; these groups advocate cultural diversity, human rights, environmental protection, and the like. Essentially, these aspects are manifestations of "socialism with a human face," such that Americans are now unknowingly and gradually living in accordance with Marxist ideals.[7]

---

6 Anatoliy Golitsyn, The Perestroika Deception (New York: Ed Harle, 1995); Ion Pacepa and Ronald J. Rychlak, Disinformation (Washington, DC: WND Books, Inc., 2013).

7 Dr. Ezepchuk interviews, 2015–2016.

The United States of America is currently under siege and has been for quite some time. Since the 1960s, American police officers have fought an increasingly intense asymmetrical war on the front lines in addition to their traditional law-enforcement duties and responsibilities. American psychological and social consciousness is a primary field of battle that manifests in various forms of confrontation and has divided the nation on a number of levels, including socially, racially, religiously, economically, and politically. Another issue is that terrorist cells are a thing of the past. Today, America and the rest of the West face a collective of decentralized terrorist armies and individual soldiers with no visible connections to terrorist organizations. Ultimately, global revolutionary dynamics are manifesting locally at an alarming rate.

According to my acquaintance from a graduate-level international security course at a university in Moscow, the overwhelming majority of aspects of international relations are controlled from behind the scenes by the special services (intelligence and security services) of the world's most influential nations; these facets include terrorism, transnational crime, cyberwarfare, the mass migration of refugees, and major social and "democratic" movements. An important fact to take into consideration regarding international and Islamic terrorism is that they are tactics in the global revolution to overthrow American capitalism and the democratic way of life, particularly right here in the homeland. No terrorist group can undertake an attack without some type of collaboration from the special services of major global players.

Decentralized and international criminal (Russian organized crime groups in particular) and terrorist networks were created and facilitated by the KGB as part of a "fifth column" during the Soviet era. Another transnational criminal organization involved with terrorism with communist roots is the MS-13 "gang" mentioned earlier. According to my law enforcement experience, I discovered that MS-13 works very closely with the Russian mafia and (subsequently) the aforementioned Russian special services. This operational activity was accomplished in conjunction with the other intelligence and security services of anti-American countries throughout Europe, Asia, Africa, and Latin America that were established with the assistance of the KGB, since socialism and communism are global revolutionary movements that spread socialist-oriented solidarity in order to eliminate American capitalism and the alleged double standards of our political leadership. Keep in mind that this process of creating illicit networks occurred when there were not nearly as many global issues and conflicts as there are today. Given the cover of the overabundance of global issues and conflicts today, just think what Russia and its allies can achieve.

Officers, agents, and informants of the Russian special services are without a doubt the most capable, creative, intelligent, and innovative warriors on the planet. They are experts at conducting insurrectionary operations effectively and clandestinely in unstable conditions to such a degree that any connections they may have to Russia are invisible. Ultimately, the Russian special services and their members are true warriors in every sense of the word and should never be underestimated.

It is very important to understand that Russia's continuous undermining of the United States stems from the Russian Revolution of 1917, which is an ongoing global revolution. Maintaining the constant state of revolution globally is critical to the success of Marxism-Leninism (and Chekism, a condition in Soviet and post-Soviet society in which the security and intelligence services control all aspects of the country including people, businesses, government, industries, all forms of media, literature, films, dissident movements, the political and economic system, the educational system and so on) and to this day has been quite successful. In fact, Marxism-Leninism is the primary driving force behind all major global issues as responses to American neoliberalism. The proof lies in the current state of international affairs and, even worse, the current situation in America. At the same time, the Russian leadership collective of Chekists—Putin's junta—has done an outstanding job of minimizing the threat that the Russian FSB (Federal Security Service) and SVR (Foreign Intelligence Service) pose to the United States; through Russia's various agents of influence, the junta has conditioned us to look at Islamic terrorist organizations as our main threat.

Today, America's enemies are living among us and have been for quite some time, thanks to lax immigration laws that proliferated via the school of thought that America is a nation of immigrants—as, of course, we are. An unfortunate example was the 9/11 hijackers, who exploited America's concept of itself as a nation of immigrants. These individuals came to the United States under the typical notion of pursuing the American Dream when in reality they had hostile intentions. America is indeed a nation of immigrants; but because we are at war, maintaining a naive perception of global dynamics with porous borders and allowing large flows of immigrants—both of which are ideal for terrorists and transnational criminals to blend into—is detrimental in the long run. The continuation of this process will only lead to the further collapse of the United States. Unfortunately, there is no way to identify illicit individuals from those who have good intentions within the waves of immigrants to the United States annually. In dealing with immigration, American leadership must understand that we are at war and that our national sovereignty is at stake; as such, the act of hiring naturalized citizens who are native or heritage speakers of languages critical to US national security to work in the US government in any capacity is a strategic and tactical mistake.

It was pointed out to me at one of the universities I studied at in Moscow that the timing of the dissolution of the USSR and the Warsaw Pact nations was rather intriguing. In the late 1980s and early 1990s, the "Washington consensus" (which was essentially the complete deregulation of capitalism and a goal of Russia's modern version of Lenin's New Economic Policy of the 1920s) was also taking shape; it evolved into what is known today as American neoliberalism. Briefly speaking, the university taught that neoliberalism is unregulated capitalism that wishes to maximize profit at *any* cost, even the well-being and day-to-day survivability of the common worker. Any restrictions to the flow of goods and services are lifted under neoliberalism. At this time, American jobs began to be outsourced, and the citizens of developing nations were exploited by working long hours for very little pay. It was a lose-lose situation for the average person, both in America and globally, while corporate executives got rich. Meanwhile, there was a strong basis for renewed anti-Americanism. People are *legally* exploited by other people so that top-level managers can accumulate capital and maximize profit in addition to looking out for shareholder interests while negating the people who are making the profit possible—the average workers—even in the United States. American neo-liberalism is the driving force behind wage stagnation, unemployment, and underemployment.[8]

Putin called the collapse of the USSR the greatest tragedy of the twentieth century. But it is also important to note that (according to Russian culture) out of the worst tragedies come the greatest triumphs. The concepts of the dissolution of the USSR and the end of the Cold War are of tremendous importance. Essentially, the relatively stable yet fragile balance of a bipolar world immediately ceased to exist after the dissolution of the Soviet Union. Decentralized and illicit structures formed by the KGB during the Soviet period led to an increase in global instability and a rise in local, regional, and international conflicts; a large number of terrorist attacks; and human migration on an unprecedented scale. The Soviets also knew that the dissolution of the USSR would break the bipolar stability and send Muslims and "former" communists alike around the world, thus advancing not only the communist Russian Revolution that began in 1917 but also the Islamic Iranian Revolution that began in 1979. Again, both of these revolutions continue to this day.

Interestingly, at the same time that *perestroika* (restructuring) was occurring, the USSR implemented a law called "On Co-operatives in the USSR" on May 26, 1988, with periodic amendments through April 15, 1998—despite the so-called dissolution of the Soviet Union. This legislation was in accordance with the constitution of the USSR (even in 1998);

---

8 Underemployment mainly occurs when highly qualified people have low-paying jobs: part-time jobs that are created so that firms can avoid providing benefits and higher pay. Wage stagnation, unemployment, and underemployment against the background of increases in costs of living has fueled the global communist movement. The best thing that private businesses can do is to start taking care of their employees in order to weaken communist influence. This unfortunately means sacrificing profit, but it is an absolutely necessary maneuver that they must do in the name of national security.

it defines the economic, social, and legal conditions for the activities of co-operatives on the foundation of the development of Lenin's ideas applied to the modern stage of the construction of socialism in the USSR. Essentially, co-operative legislation is a modified form of Lenin's New Economic Policy, which allows capitalism on the surface when, in reality, the state is still in control.[9] The KGB was and continues to be tasked with managing and controlling all business on the territory of the former Soviet Union. KGB agents and high-ranking Communist Party officials (and relatives) were appointed to be "entrepreneurs" and "businessmen" of the most profitable industries, including natural resources, technology, defense, and the like. This practice provides proof that oligarchs were either KGB or very closely connected to the KGB and/or high-ranking Communist Party of the Soviet Union (CPSU) officials. A modern example is the appointment of the son of former FSB Director Nikolai Patrushev, Andrei Patrushev, to the administration of Gazprom (formerly known as the Soviet Ministry of Gas). At just twenty-five, the younger Patrushev had been previously appointed to the administration of Rosneft (formerly known as the Soviet Ministry of Oil and Gas). It is important to note that these Soviet entities have remained operational under new names despite the dissolution of the USSR. Essentially, this dynamic continues to be hidden by highly sophisticated disinformation operations and other smokescreens that mask a system with certain similarities to the Chinese economic model, which is also based on Marxism-Leninism. The very concept of China—a Marxist-Leninist-Maoist nation soon to be the world's largest economy—is frightening. So much for communism being an unviable system and ideology of the past.

Supporting these operations is the process of achieving global governance via a plethora of international and regional organizations staffed with graduates of the leftist/liberal/socialist Peoples' Friendship University, a Russian university that educates students to be effective in the revolutionary internationalization movement in order to construct a multipolar world through the promotion of humanitarian and scientific

9 Golitsyn, The Perestroika Deception, 1995, pp. 80-84.

progress. A "multipolar world" is a term used to signify that America is not the global leader but rather that several nations are of equal importance in leading international affairs. The Peoples' Friendship University advances the communist goal of replacing nation-states and their governments with global, regional, and local organizations that are specific to defined issues related to diplomacy, environmental issues, the sciences and humanities, technology, social-justice issues, transnational crime and terrorism, and human-rights issues. The Peoples' Friendship University is a member of the International Forum of Public Universities, which, according to my Russian colleagues, educates future leaders in international socialist and revolutionary ideals. At the time of writing of this book, the official site to this organization is unfortunately inaccessible, but hopefully not for long. The US government can no longer keep up with all of these problems itself: it has no other alternative than to rely on organizations and to outsource contractors to work at solving problems.[10]

Communist Russia's unification with the Muslim world was and continues to be fueled by the global struggle against Western imperialism, individualism, and double standards. Large components of the Soviet Union and post-Soviet space are Muslims, so this "unification" was deemed necessary. In order to understand modern Russia and its role in international affairs, it is crucial to take a very close look at its fascinating and intriguing cultural history. In Russian culture, the past is merged into the present and future, thus rendering history, symbols, and traditions extremely important, particularly from generation to generation. A significant period of this cultural history occurred when Russia was part of the Mongolian Empire as that empire's course of development became rooted in expansionism, military conquest, militant government structure, and maintaining a powerful Asian despotic leadership style focused on security, diplomacy, and intelligence. An interesting side note is that during the time when Russia was part of the Mongolian Empire (1240–1480), Islam became an integral part of Russian society. To this day, the Russian

---

10 One goal of communism is to eliminate government and to govern via international organizations and international institutions.

government's reason for existence is to wage war, control global processes of development and resources, and expand its areas of influence, just as the Golden Horde had done. This cultural-historical component eventually led to Russia's conquest of Central Asia and its subsequent manipulation of and unification with the Muslim world during the Soviet period of Russian history.

CHAPTER 1

The Modern Russian
System of State Security

• • •

In this chapter, I will present the highlights of notes I took during meetings with a Russian graduate student whom I met while studying abroad. This student was kind enough to show me around the university we studied at (as well as Moscow in general); we had several very interesting conversations over coffee at the McDonald's near Moscow's Tverskaya Metro Station every Saturday morning during the winter and spring quarters of 2013. He was also an expert in Russia-China relations who was fluent in Mandarin Chinese. His career aspirations included becoming a government official or a military intelligence officer specializing in economic warfare. We had several fascinating discussions and debates on relations between the United States and Russia. I often took the position that it is necessary for Russia and the United States to work together in order to learn about Russian strategy because I knew that Russia, China, and the rest of the socialist world are striving to eliminate the United States as a significant global player in all aspects of global affairs. This student agreed with me and said that the transformation has been underway for quite some time and that there was no other alternative. The following section consists of the information from our meetings.

THE FUNDAMENTAL PRIORITIES IN RUSSIA's concept of its national security are national defense, state security, and public security. In May of 2007, a conference took place in which leading academics from the Russian Academy of Sciences discussed the findings of several studies and various socioeconomic experiments in the field of national security. The conference determined Russia's new national security strategy for the twenty-first century, which is centered upon economic security and peaceful diplomacy. The Russian Academy of Sciences is interwoven into the special services as a research and analysis entity that helps formulate the nation's domestic and foreign policy. This entity also strives to formulate ideas within American think tanks in order to influence our foreign policy with all nations from the former Soviet Union.

It should be noted that genuine security is not just a matter of ensuring order and the protection of the ruling elite: security also entails the ability and desire to secure the evolutionary and stable development of society, including the ability of state security agencies to support this type of total progressive development.

Russia's Security Council, which is composed of top state officials, is in charge of the nation's entire system of state security, including the country's special services. The Security Council concentrates its activities on preparing decisions for the president in a diverse range of objectives to ensure the security of the country. The prototype of the Russian Security Council was the Security Council of the USSR, which was entrusted with making recommendations for implementing Soviet policies, which included assuring national defense, economic and environmental security, and societal stability and maintaining the country's robustness while dealing with the consequences of natural disasters and other emergencies—to name a few. In 1991, before the dissolution of the USSR, each Soviet republic completed the organization of its own Security Council and system of state security, which mirrored that of the Russian Federation. Russian special service officers served in the special services of all of the former Soviet republics in order to maintain consistency and continuity in running these independent nations after assisting them in preparing for the Soviet Union's transition to the aforementioned Commonwealth of Independent States (CIS). Of course, this process was accompanied by amending or rewriting the constitutions of each independent republic of the USSR. An internal organization of the CIS of great significance is the Shanghai Cooperation Organization (SCO), which adds China and other major players to an increasingly influential organization that has received very little attention from the West.[11]

The overarching goal of the 2016 SCO summit was to increase its global influence in order to establish a multipolar world order led by Russia and China rather than the United States. I find it very interesting that "Brexit" (Great Britain's proposed exit from the European Union) "suddenly" was finalized at the same time the SCO summit was taking place. Brexit is an anti-capitalist maneuver designed to facilitate class struggles and geopolitical instability supported by the British section of the International Committee of the Fourth International, which is maneuvering to overthrow capitalism and replace the European Union with the United Socialist States of Europe.[12]

Russia is in charge of the Fourth International (known as the Comintern), which is currently supervised by a division of the FSB known as the International Partnership Directorate, formerly known as the International Liaison Department (or OMS in Russian). Because communism is a global movement, the Western hemisphere is next, since Russia and China are in complete control of Eurasia. Correspondingly, Brexit is a textbook example of Hegelian dialectics in action and is a significant step toward the construction of a global system of state communism in accordance with Russia, China, and India. Ultimately, the possible connection of Brexit with the SCO needs to be explored and analyzed, particularly in

---

11 One of the main functions of the SCO is the unification of anti-imperialist nations that are composed mostly of member, observer, and dialogue partner nations from the former communist world in the formation of a parallel global economy separate from the American-led economy. The ultimate goal is to replace American hegemony in all spheres, from financial-economic to humanitarian, cultural, and political-military. This school of thought is essentially the foundation of the multipolar world that Russia and China are in the process of establishing. This process began during the Soviet period and gained momentum with the dissolution of the USSR and its subsequent reorganization into the CIS.

12 https://www.wsws.org/en/articles/2016/02/29/pers-f29.html.

the spheres of economics and energy partnerships, since the SCO works closely with the European Union.

In general, the special services are commonly understood to be public authorities that have been established and operate in the interest of protecting the interests and national security of various nations, both domestically and internationally. They have always been at the forefront of the struggle against American capitalism; they provide political leadership around the globe with objective and reliable information about the actual state of affairs in any spheres of sociopolitical and economic life that require solutions of the utmost competence.

The components of Russia's system of state security, as was explained to me, consists of a series of structures and organs that include the armed forces; federal security and migration services; foreign intelligence; emergency rescue services; civil defense units; border security forces; organs of industrial-complex security, energy sites, natural-resource security, and of internal affairs and forces, and many others. In addition, there are top-secret agencies no one even knows exist.

The core ministries and departments of the Russian system of state security are the Ministry of Internal Affairs, the Ministry of Civil Defense, the Ministry of Emergency Services, the Ministry of Foreign Affairs, the Ministry of Defense, the Ministry of Justice, the Foreign Intelligence Service, the aforementioned Federal Security Service (FSB), the Federal Protection Service, and the Main Administration of Special Programs of the President. Ultimately, the majority of the national security burden lies on the FSB, which is the core of the Russian system of state security. The sword-and-shield symbol of the FSB represents the defense of the global communist revolution by any means necessary while putting the enemy to death. The FSB is not simply the KGB renamed but rather the heart of an elaborate and progressive system of state security.

Counterintelligence departments of the FSB are engaged in the protection of the constitutional order and the fight against terrorism, which includes analysis, forecasting, and strategic planning. The FSB has its own special forces (just like the Iranian Revolutionary Guard Corps), which operate from the Special Operations Center in Moscow under the Department of Counterterrorism and consists of two special forces— Alpha (a counterterror group) and Vympel. The FSB Special Forces also has members that are inactive yet still operational.

Vympel is a special forces unit that originated as a tactical operative arm of the KGB Foreign Intelligence Directorate, currently known as the SVR (as noted earlier, the Foreign Intelligence Service). Vympel was formed under the direction of KGB general Yuri Drozdov; its primary functions are to fight terrorism; free hostages; guard strategically important facilities such as nuclear facilities, military factories, and airports; engage in sabotage; protect spies, who operate under the cover of businessmen and embassy workers; cause train derailments, engage in mountain warfare and start forest fires (please see photos in appendix) and fires at chemical plants, and so on. It is well known by security professionals that fires are one of the worst disasters to affect a nation's resources due to the amount of resources that are required to extinguish them and from the aggregate damages that can occur. Vympel also helps to train guerillas who are engaged in fighting American forces by assisting in the formation of terrorist organizations and by training those organizations to conduct terrorist attacks. During peacetime, Vympel is also tasked with identifying security weaknesses in facilities ranging from airports and industrial sites to banks and business and sports complexes. Vympel operatives are usually fluent in at least two foreign languages, possess superior skills in combat sambo (a Russian martial art focusing on self-defense without weapons) and survival skills, and generally are the best of the best because they *have* to do everything better than anyone else.

The Ministry of Internal Affairs (MVD) ensures public safety through the protection of public order and the prevention, detection, and suppression of all types of crime. The duties, functions, and responsibilities of the MVD (and its subunits) can be modified at any time in accordance with Russian federal law No. 3-F3 "On Police," which went into effect on March 1, 2011. MVD divisions also include the nationwide police force, investigators, traffic police, and traffic accident investigations divisions. A military police unit was also recently established that serves similar functions as in the US armed forces.

The MVD also has its own army in addition to regular officers, including police special forces units that consist of: 1) A separate division of special forces (ODON); 2) special forces regiment *Vityaz*; and 3) special forces detachments *Lynx*, *Rosich*, *Scythian*, and *Peresvet*. The category of military units of the MVD also includes regional divisions OMON (police special forces) and SOBR (special rapid reaction unit). As of April 5, 2016, MVD Special Forces, along with private security officers, were reorganized into what is known as the National Guard.

The Foreign Intelligence Service (SVR) works with the military intelligence division of foreign intelligence—the Main Intelligence Directorate (GRU)—in conducting information-support activities in the protection of national security, counterterrorism operations both domestically and internationally, and the protection of families of service members both domestically and internationally. The GRU also has an economic warfare division that works closely with the SVR. These services also collect and analyze information on the activities of foreign and international organizations by becoming members or consultants of the organization(s). The SVR has its own special forces unit, known as *Zaslon*, which consists of agents, officers, and informants from all of the former Soviet republics. Its members have become citizens of the country they operate in (primarily the United States) and have US passports.

The Russian Ministry of Defense is responsible for providing protection of Russia (via the manufacturing and use of WMDs, missiles and small arms, and ammunition and explosives) and of military facilities. The ministry also takes part in securing national maritime traffic and the airspace of the Russian Federation. It consists of the army, navy, strategic missile forces, air and space force, and airborne forces.

It is crucial to understand that the Russian system of state security is constantly evolving and reorganizing to meet various global and domestic security challenges. The process of social development is such that it continuously faces one controversy or conflict after another as the global communist revolution mutates into different forms. After major challenges have been solved or are no longer effective, other challenges and threats to the national security of foreign nations are developed and implemented; at times they are radically different in form and content than the previous challenge. In doing so, Russia develops countermeasures to address possible responses. This practice ensures that Russia remains many steps ahead of the United States in all aspects of international relations.

CHAPTER 2

The Soviet Exploitation
of Islam and Muslims

• • •

This entire chapter is based on my discussions with Dr. Ezepchuk from
2015 to 2016 unless otherwise noted.

IN ORDER TO ATTRACT SUPPORT for the global communist uprising, the
Soviets manipulated and exploited the political ideology of Islam and
Muslims beginning in approximately 1905, shortly after the first Russian
Revolution. Soviet leaders knew that proliferating political Islam and enlist-
ing the support of Muslims for the Soviet regime was invaluable to firmly
establishing the world's first socialist nation. The Soviets also knew that
conducting this type of sociocultural experiment was not going to be easily
accomplished; they knew it was absolutely necessary, however, since the
overwhelming masses of Muslims in Siberia, Russian Turkestan, and the
Caucasus region were experiencing oppression and exploitation under
the Russian Empire. This condition proved to be a very strong platform
in bringing this strategy to fruition. Therefore, since the early days of the
Soviets' seizing of control and establishment of the Soviet government, its
leaders considered Islam as a future ally in the global revolution against free-
market capitalism, Western imperialism, and American-style democracy.

Lenin and Trotsky were confident that bolshevism would successfully liberate the entire East—from the Middle East to China and even
what is now Indonesia—and eventually would lead to the entire Muslim

world leading a permanent revolution on a global scale through a pan-Islamic global revolution.[13] Lenin was confident that Soviet propaganda, by spreading the pitfalls and inherent destructive socioeconomic effects of capitalism on a society while promoting anti-Westernism and anti-imperialism, would attract the support of millions of people.

Among these tremendous masses of people on the Eurasian continent, Islam was the predominant "religion" of nearly five hundred million; in the early 1920s, there were approximately thirty million Muslims in the Soviet Union. The ultimate goal of the bolsheviks was clear: to manipulate and use the world of Islam in the worldwide struggle against the West and its interests and to acquire the natural resources of sovereign nations. One pillar of the Soviet position in this matter rests upon how the West, especially the United States and Great Britain, exploited the people of sovereign nations in order to maintain access to and control and transportation of natural resources.

The foundation (and facilitation) of the strategy of manipulating Muslims was centered around three spiritual directorates of Muslims in the Soviet Union. All Islamic functions and activities in Russian society were controlled by the Departmental Commission on Cults in the All-Russian Central Committee, which was supervised by the Cheka. Their work was directed by the politburo of the Communist Party of the Soviet Union (CPSU). Essentially, a two-faith system was developed and implemented. The first faith was atheism, which demanded the recognition of and submission to Soviet symbols,[14] and the second was Islam. Interestingly, the Soviet-style atheism inherent to the moral code of the builders of communism is based upon Christian principles and the Sermon on the Mount. Briefly speaking, the moral code of 1961 is based on twelve commandments on how communists are to conduct their lives in connection to the conceptual strategy of socialism with a human face.

---

13   This strategy was continued by the KGB in forming the PLO and assisting Iran during the Iranian (Islamic) Revolution. Today it is ISIS and in the future it will be yet another organization.

14   This factor is a primary reason that Soviet symbols remain to this day throughout the former Soviet Union.

The commandments highlight workers' ethics, solidarity of the global communist movement with brother socialist and communist nations (and/or their people who live in capitalist countries), and intolerance toward the enemies of communism—capitalists. The moral code is the foundation of the creation of a new, progressive, and most advanced type of human in the history of mankind—*Homo sovieticus.*[15]

Despite the well-organized structural control mechanisms in place, political mistakes by Soviet diplomats and their propaganda following the First Congress of the Peoples of the East, which took place in 1920 in Baku, Azerbaijan, caused problems. Complicating matters further, many Islamic countries were still under control and/or influence of the West, from Western Asia to the Indonesian archipelago. These obstacles made the sovietization process of these peoples nearly impossible. Due to the previously mentioned aspects, hostility toward communism and the USSR in general manifested and needed to be addressed. Fortunately, the Muslims in the Soviet Union still remembered how the Soviets had liberated them from the oppression and exploitation they had experienced under the rule of the Russian Empire. Of course, installing Muslims in key leadership positions in Islamic regions of the USSR was also a significant factor in controlling and/or crushing any type of revolt. A similar type of process is well underway in the United States: traditional American culture, which is based on Christian principles, is eroding and being replaced with socialism as key positions in American society are infiltrated by those with leftist orientations. Exacerbating matters is the toll that unregulated capitalism (neoliberalism) is having on the American people as the gap between the wealthy and the poor widens on an unprecedented scale in American history thanks to the ingenious operations of socialists and communists infiltrating corporate America and advocating deregulation in as many spheres of business as possible.

Shortly after the Russian Revolution of 1917, complete religious freedom was established for Muslims in the former Russian Empire. Lenin and other Soviet leaders were very cautious in how they related

---

15 Dr. Ezepchuk interviews, 2015–2016.

to Muslims, including their customs and traditions both public and private. The Soviets were also open-minded and flexible in how they collaborated with the Muslim populations during the Russian Civil War (1917–1922), while the Soviet regime simultaneously launched waves of terror against Orthodox Christians. We must remember, however, that at that time, the Soviet government had yet to be firmly established. As it turned out, the Muslims discovered that the proclamation of religious freedom and the Soviet support of Islam were nothing but lies and deception meant to attract support from a very large portion of the population of the USSR. Of course, this supportive position toward the Islamic world would soon change once the Soviets achieved their goal of coming to power.

From 1929 to 1941, the Soviets launched another repressive terror campaign against all religions, including Islam. Mosques were destroyed, and many Muslims were repressed and/or forcibly exiled to Siberia, since all religions were deemed to be nothing but cults that impeded the social and technological progress of the recently established Soviet nation. The Chekists of the OGPU and NKVD (early names for the KGB) were in complete control of this process.

The Third Communist International (1919–1943), known as the Comintern, was an international organization that proclaimed that there were at least four times the number of people in Asia than in Europe and how crucial it was to be flexible and open-minded in fomenting communist revolutions in nations such as China, India, Turkey, and Persia in order to increase the chances of establishing world communism and to launch the process of replacing the state with various international and regional organizations. Upon the dissolution of the Soviet Union, these masses of people could more easily emigrate to the West to become influential forces in capitalist countries in all societal capacities. Lenin and the Soviets knew that in the East, religion and spirituality were extremely important to people, so a creative approach to entice interest in joining the global communist revolution was necessary. This consideration is also why the Soviet moral code was/is composed of religious elements. At the same time, strategy and tactics were needed to awaken the working class and to drive them to the point of hostility toward the bourgeoisie throughout the world with the will to fight wealthy, exploitive, and oppressive Western capitalists. The ultimate goal was to transform every individual Muslim into a *Homo sovieticus*. This is where the art and science of teaching agitators to agitate gained momentum—not only in the Islamic world but also throughout the third world and even in the United States—beginning in the 1960s. Racism and religious confrontation are often the most popular methods of direct action to be applied in this aspect.

Eventually, the Cheka strategy of militarizing and radicalizing Islam against the West resulted in the mutation of many Islamic terrorist organizations. Today, with the assistance of strategic propaganda, groups such as Al-Qaeda and IS/ISIS dominate rhetoric in the media. This tactic takes focus away from the true propellants of global Islamic terrorism: the Russian special services and the Iranian Revolutionary Guard Corps (IRGC).

CHAPTER 3

A Brief Word on the Iranian Special Services

• • •

This chapter is based on my lecture notes from my international security course and from notes I obtained during discussions with my Russian contact in Moscow. The Iranian special forces are close partners of the Russian Federal Security Service (FSB) and the Russian Foreign Intelligence Service (SVR).

TODAY, IRAN'S POLITICAL INTELLIGENCE, THE Ministry of Information, is operational in more than forty countries around the world, including the United States, and plays a significant role in facilitating transnational crime and terrorism. The ministry is tasked with the creation of clandestine intelligence and revolutionary terrorist networks in North and South America, Africa, and the Middle East, with the assistance of the Russian FSB and SVR. The FSB and SVR, according to my contact, are operational in at least 140 nations and operate closely with the special services of the Organisation of Islamic Cooperation (OIC),[16] including the OIC's member nations and observer nations. These networks are planned to be used in the event that the United States' presence in these countries begins to pose an imminent threat to Iran or Iranian interests abroad.

---

16 All nations associated with the OIC are enemies of the United States. The perception that some of these nations are allies of America are the result of successful disinformation operations.

The Quds Force is the strike brigade of the global Iranian (Islamic) revolution, just as the Cheka is the strike brigade for the global communist revolution. Their main task is to prepare and conduct terrorist acts and operations in any region of the planet in coordination with the Russian FSB and SVR. The Quds Force, in conjunction with the Russian FSB and SVR, played a significant role in the strategic planning of 9/11, according to my contact. Of course, the FSB spreads conspiracy theories that the CIA was responsible for deflecting the FSB's involvement.[17]

The Iranian special services utilize the tactic of sleeping agents, a practice developed and perfected by the KGB. Students are recruited and trained and then emigrate to the West (to places such as the United States or Western Europe), where they "fall asleep." These intelligence operatives get married, have children, become US citizens, and lead lives as law-abiding citizens while awaiting instructions from the center. In the event of any type of attack on Iran, Russia, China, or any of their strategic partners, sleeper agents in the West are ready to attack the United States and/or its European NATO allies.

The code name of this joint operation of Russia, China, and Iran— with support from over a hundred strategic partner countries, military forces, and transnational criminal and terrorist organizations (including MS-13, drug cartels, and street gangs)—is believed to be *judgment day*. In fact, the strategy in which terrorists operate within and with street gangs and drug cartels is meant to further destabilize society, disable as many people as possible through drug addiction, and overwhelm the judicial and health-care systems; their strategy is not simply to be a source of financing for terrorist operations, as is often misconstrued as the sole reason for this nexus. Societal destabilization by any and all means is an

---

17 Slandering and/or discrediting individuals and organizations alike are key tactics of the FSB and SVR. According to Golitsyn, 1995, the KGB came up with the term "cold warriors" to identify Americans who question perestroika, the collapse of communism, and dissolution of the USSR. Because of this factor, American political, economic, business, and educational leaders believed the KGB was telling the truth and no investigation was conducted. Now, we all are paying the price as the United States is increasingly under communist control.

overarching goal that is becoming increasingly successful here in the United States.

According to my contact, the organizational structure of the Quds Force consists of eleven directorates, as follows.

1. **The Directorate for Southern Russia (including the Caucasus), Black Sea and Caspian Sea Regions** assists Russia in facilitating the tactic of transnational crime in this region; assisted in the experiment forming an Islamic state in Chechnya as a prototype for the IS today; the division also supports and communicates with the Hezbollah movement in Turkey, the Kurdistan Workers' Party (Marxists-Leninists), the Turkish Islamic Opposition Party, and the Islamic Party of Azerbaijan. It is imperative to understand that Hezbollah is not simply an Iranian-Lebanese terrorist organization and political party; it is also a Marxist-Leninist-Islamic movement that is present from Lebanon to Pakistan and is connected to the Gulen/Hizmet movement from Turkey.

2. **The Directorate for Iraq** provides assistance and support Hezbollah in Iraq and works with the Supreme Council for Islamic Revolution in Iraq, including various parties and anti-American resistance groups.

3. **The Directorate for Lebanon, the West Bank, and the Gaza Strip** works and provides comprehensive assistance movements to Amal, Hezbollah, Hamas, and the Islamic Jihad Organization. Agents and officers play an active role in combat operations under the guise of various Islamist movements.

4. **The Directorate for Kazakhstan, Kyrgyzstan, Tajikistan, Uzbekistan, Turkmenistan, Afghanistan, Pakistan, and India, a.k.a. the Central and Southern Asia Directorate**, works and provides close support to Islamic and social movements and Islamic parties in the republics of Central Asia as well as clandestine social movements to counter US attempts at any type of influence in the region. In Afghanistan, this directorate consults and assists

the Islamic Society of Afghanistan, the National Islamic Front of Afghanistan, the National Front for the Rescue of Afghanistan, the Islamic Union for the Liberation of Afghanistan, the Party for Islamic Unity in Afghanistan, the National Islamic Movement of Afghanistan, and the Taliban. In Pakistan, it supports the Islamic social movement Amal (a Marxist-Leninist movement) and the Movement of the Islamic Revolution of Kashmir.

5. **The Directorate for North Africa** supports Islamic groups in Algeria, Libya, Tunisia, Egypt, Sudan, and South Sudan to counter US influence on the continent. Of all these nations, Iran sees Sudan as a stronghold/platform for the Iranian-Shiite expansion in Africa. In Sudan and South Sudan, Iran operates special training centers for Islamic militants, who then emigrate to the United States under lottery programs. The main activity of this directorate is the recruitment of Arab and African youth to conduct combat, reconnaissance, and special operations in the interests of Iran as well as the dissemination of ideas of the Islamic revolution throughout the world. This directorate played a significant role in the attack on the American embassy in Benghazi, Libya, in 2012.

6. **The Directorate for the Western Hemisphere** focuses on the spreading of Islamic organizations (both Shiite and Sunni) and socio-Islamic movements; the placing of refugees and immigrants from Iraq, North Africa, Iraq, and Syria into the West; and promoting the placement of students, interns, and scientists into Western educational programs for intelligence operations in conjunction with Russia, Cuba, and China. This directorate is also responsible for intelligence operations, the recruitment of agents and militants to carry out terrorist acts, the exportation of ideas of the global Islamic revolution, and of course the proliferation of the idea of a global Islamic state. It promotes social movements and organizations in the United States with the FSB and SVR among African Americans, including the Nation of Islam, the Black Lives Matter movement, and the New Black Panthers (all of which are based on Marxism-Leninism and are designed to destabilize American society).

7. **The Directorate for Central and South Africa** accomplishes its work mainly through Iranian cultural and Islamic centers, diplomatic missions, mosques, Shia communities, and Islamic schools in this region. The directorate has been most active in Somalia, Kenya, Chad and Nigeria (via Boko Haram), Zambia, Burkina Faso, and Senegal.

8. **The Directorate for the Persian Gulf Region** supports the Shiite community in the region and is connected to the Organization of the Ulema (in Saudi Arabia) and Hezbollah in Bahrain.

9. **The Directorate for Syria** supports the Assad regime in partnership with Russia and works closely with the Western Hemisphere directorate. Agents in this directorate also infiltrate opposition groups that the United States supports and trains.

10. **The Economic Warfare Directorate** focuses on utilizing Poland, the Balkans, and the former Czechoslovakia as trading partners to circumvent sanctions.

11. **The Quds Global Cyber Directorate** is essentially an extension of the Russian FSB's Scientific-Technical Services Directorate and Chinese Cyber Warfare Forces; it also works closely with North Korean cyberexperts. In technological spheres, Iran has tremendous potential in the export of scientific-technical, engineering, and information technology (IT) services, especially in the event that sanctions are lifted. One of Iran's most important commercial business strategies is to export modern high-tech industrial products; Iranian entrepreneurs want to enter the European market through Poland, the Czech Republic and Slovakia, Hungary, and the former Yugoslavia. All Iranians in these countries are conducting some type of intelligence operation, often under the cover of embassies or legitimate businesses (such as restaurants or hotels). If the United States were to lift sanctions on Iran, that nation would certainly become a regional superpower, since it would then have access to billions of dollars of previously frozen financial assets.

CHAPTER 4

The Foundation of Putin's Russia

• • •

This entire chapter (on Marxism-Leninism, Chekism, and the Cold War) is based on my discussions with Dr. Ezepchuk from 2015 to 2016 unless otherwise noted.

SINCE VLADIMIR PUTIN IS A product of the KGB, Marxism-Leninism (M-L), and the Chekist system, it is important to analyze and discuss these factors as the first step in formulating effective foreign policy to deal with Putin's Russia, a.k.a. Putin's junta. The events and dynamics that occurred during the Soviet period of Russian history are now having a profound effect on the modern global community, particularly the United States. The world we live in is not as complex as we are led to believe by the media, educators, and politicians if one views global situations through the lens of Chekism. Chekism is a form of purified and radicalized M-L of the political police, intelligence, and security services that focuses on armed insurrection and revolution, state-supported terrorism (including technological terrorism), and various forms of peaceful social-liberation movements. All of these factors are tactics to maintain the constant state of global revolution. In discussions with Dr. Ezepchuk, I ascertained that M-L is much more than a planned economy and ideology.

M-L is the result of the irreversible movement of advanced scientific thought. It represents the greatest revolutionary upheaval of the entire global community in its evolutionary development—one that continues to be achieved through a variety of means. Furthermore, the Cheka is much more than another name for the KGB. The Cheka is also composed of secret elements that complete the system of state security, thus enabling the entire system to work like a fine-tuned machine. These elements are completely hidden, and their tasks are unfathomable to a normal human being. Two such areas include experimental medicine (including poisoning foods with chemicals and disease-causing agents) and experimental psychology, the latter of which involves achieving mind control over individuals to force them to commit murder or suicide, become active shooters, blow themselves up, or to do anything else that may be desired of them, including altering the morals and perceptions of who the enemy is in individuals and society alike.

This section of the book is intended to provide a theoretical foundation of the modern Russian strategy and foreign policy that is indeed centered upon Marxism-Leninism, despite rhetoric to the contrary. It is of utmost importance to comprehend the concept that modern terrorism and various liberation movements are based on the violent ideology and revolutionary concepts of M-L and Chekism. In fact, truly comprehending the entire scope of Putin's Russia; international Islamic terrorism; and the socioeconomic, cultural, and political conditions in the United States today would be impossible without having a firm grasp of the tenets of Marxism-Leninism and, subsequently, Chekism. These factors are the key to understanding and dealing with Russia and its allies.

Contrary to popular discourse, Marxism-Leninism is alive and well in the former Soviet Union and other Warsaw Pact nations, China, Latin America, and so on. One part of the Chekist strategy was transferring the global socialist revolution to the third world, which includes Africa, the Islamic world, and Latin America. A solid comprehension of the basics of M-L and Chekism is also essential for simplifying international relations today, which are generally considered to be complex. The reality is that if one has a solid grasp on M-L, modern global issues and dynamics are actually quite simple. One of the reasons the United States is unable to effectively deal with Russia and its allies is rooted in our lack of understanding of Marxism-Leninism and Chekism and their militant strategy to destroy American democracy, Western capitalism, and ultimately every aspect of traditional American society.

Of course, Marxism-Leninism has been rendered a taboo term and a thing of the past in this day and age in mainstream American discourse, yet, in reality, it is more active than ever in its goal of destroying free-market capitalism and American-style democracy on a global scale in order to implement a just, socialist world government. Without understanding the aspects of the CPSU and Marxism-Leninism in relation to Russia's cultural history, it would be impossible to understand modern Russia and its global goals of establishing a multipolar world. Interestingly, despite the United States' claim to be anticommunist, we live according to Marxist principles, especially among the liberal left. These principles are centered upon cultural diversity, social justice, human and civil rights, peaceful coexistence/world peace, environmental protection, and the like.

Marxism-Leninism (along with other forms of communism such as Maoism and Juche, the official political ideology of North Korea) is essentially a scientific system of philosophical, economic, and sociopolitical views composed of the revolutionary ideology of the working class unique to all nations; the science of knowledge and the revolutionary transformation of the world; the laws of societal development, nature, human thinking, and psychology; the laws of the revolutionary fight of the working class for the overthrow of exploitive capitalism; and the creative operations and tactics of the workers in the construction of a socialist and communist global society.

Marxism as a scientific expression of the fundamental interests of the working class arose in the 1840s, when drastic antagonistic controversies began to manifest in capitalist societies. At this time, the working class, for the first time in history, became an independent sociopolitical force. Marx and Engels were the creators of the scientific ideology of the working class, which included programs, strategies, and tactics of its revolutionary struggle. They critically redefined and creatively revised mankind's achievements of previous scientific and social ideas and enriched the experience of the class struggle and revolutionary movements of the working classes.

Marxism-Leninism is the natural result of the irreversible movement of advanced human thought; it represents the greatest revolutionary upheaval in world history, both in its development and in its constant evolution. The most significant theoretical sources of Marxism are classical German philosophy,[18] English political economy, and French utopian socialism, which itself is rooted in the French Revolution (1789–1799).

The most significant trait of Marxism is that it not only explains global dynamics but also defines the conditions, paths, and means of restructuring (*perestroika*) the world order, thus transforming socialism from a utopian thought to an applied science. This phenomenon became possible as a result of the spreading of materialism in order to explain the history of society, the establishment/generation of historical materialism, and the organic connections of the creative development of materialism and dialectics.

These important processes were designed to test M-L theory against the background of slowly evolving global dynamics and globalization, which are aided by advances in technology and neoliberal economics. In order to understand the role and behavior of Russia, Iran, Cuba, China, and North Korea in international relations, it is imperative to begin with the study of M-L. The historical situation after World War II resulted in the formation of a global system of socialism, the intensification of crises of the capitalist system that occur regularly and repeatedly to this day, and the ultimately significant advancement of technology that has altered the socioeconomic construction of societies globally via the expansion of

---

18 The classic German philosophy referred to here is based on the critical theory of the Frankfurt school, which is the foundational basis of modern sociology and psychology that has been proliferated in American academics and society since the 1920s. Modern psychology in the United States today continues to be rooted in this school of thought which is designed to destroy traditional American society and culture through distorting morals, perspectives on life, and to move people towards secular thinking and away from Christian values.

the international scientific-technical revolution. A good example is how advances in the IT world minimize face-to-face interactions and involvement in the community. This technical revolution has also resulted in a dangerous over-reliance on technology in the United States. The tasks of socialist and communist construction globally require the evolution and adaptation of M-L to changing conditions through creative applications, since every nation will ultimately develop its own form of socialism on the path to communism and global governance through global organizations and international institutions. Ultimately, organizations are inherently designed to keep people united and to maintain a collective alliance with those who have similar goals of reducing the role of governments in everyday life.

Marxism was tested after emerging as the revolutionary theory of the working class, beginning with the revolutions in Western Europe in 1848–1849. This period marked the establishment of the revolutionary international party of the working class, called the International Association of Workers, under the leadership of Marx and Engels. The first International was founded on September 28, 1864. In the 1870s and 1880s, in many European countries, social-democratic and labor parties led by workers were formed on a massive scale.

The further creative development of Marxism was continued by Lenin, hence the term "Marxism-Leninism." Lenin raised the revolutionary study of Marxism to a new and higher level. Indeed, the thesis of the Central Committee of the CPSU proclaimed that "Leninism is the Marxist epoch of imperialism and proletarian revolution, the epoch of the crash of colonialism and the victory of national-liberation movements, the epoch of the transformation of mankind from capitalism to socialism, with the ultimate goal of the construction of a global communist society."

In Marxism-Leninism, society was understood for the first time as an integral social organism that can be artificially constructed and controlled; the structure of this organism can be distinguished in industrial power and relations and various defined areas of public life, including politics, law, morals, and the state/government as well as philosophy, science, art, and religion. This is why KGB officers (remember, Putin is a product of this organization), agents, and informants are necessary to control all aspects of society. Their unity and cooperation constitute society at a certain stage of history: the development and replacement of a socioeconomic and political system that is comprised of the process of progressive movement of society from capitalism to socialism and, ultimately, to communism, the most advanced form of human society. This mentality is present throughout most of the Eurasian landmass.

The core of Marxist philosophy is dialectic materialism, which serves as the common methodology of genuine scientific knowledge of both nature and society alike. The main aspects to be investigated by this philosophical school of thought include the doctrine of conflict, the law of unity, the struggle of opposites to reveal the source of social movements, and the development of the processes of reality. Lenin's contribution to the development of Marxist philosophy was centered upon socioeconomic classes, various subjective factors in the historical process, and the role of scientific theory in revolutionary movements. The researching of revolutionary theory therefore needs to be the foundation of combating modern international terrorism and subsequently Cold War–style hybrid warfare tactics. (I will use the term "cold warfare tactics" from now on.)

Marx and Engels proved that the most important driving force in the development of a society is the antagonistic struggle between socioeconomic classes. Therefore, issues such as social justice, racism, fair wages, and the like are core issues in creating and maintaining the struggle between classes (the rich and poor). In order to transform a capitalist nation (and the global community in general) into a communist one, this struggle needs to be intensified and maintained locally, regionally, and globally. This factor is a primary reason for the abundance of global strife today. In the United States, the war being waged by communist and socialist forces against our police is evidence of these dynamics right here in our own country.

Marx and Engels did not invent this idea but rather observed it as a reaction to dynamics within capitalist societies. Lenin subsequently expanded on this dynamic approach. The most realistic way and means of destroying capitalism, according to Marx and Engels, was through social-ist revolution. Lenin also determined that sometimes "peaceful, coexist-ing approaches"[19] may be necessary, depending upon global dynamics and conditions (especially regarding the United States). Transitioning to com-munism is an organic composition of socialist-intellectual revolution and terrorism.

In order to achieve socialist revolution and to establish a dictatorship of the proletariat and the destruction of all forms of exploitation of people by people, it is first necessary to liberate and unite the average exploited worker and the disenfranchised poor under the Scholastic revolutionary theory of intellectuals. Lenin also proclaimed that between the capital-ist and communist formations comes a period of transition during which, once the workers have taken control of the leadership of a nation, the po-litical police must guide and direct all aspects of public life on the path to the development of not only a new society but a new, unprecedented type of human being (later referred to as *Homo sovieticus*). Once this process is firmly established, society will advance in a new direction with only peri-odic guidance and interference needed in order to ensure that the desired course is maintained. The political police (the Cheka) assist in the facilita-tion of this process. In my opinion, this is the current condition in the United States, since it seems that this nation is currently transforming into a socialist nation in response to corporate America's flat-out attack on the average worker through low-paying jobs that demand complete and total submission and the dedication of their lives to the companies they work for through long hours (millions of Americans work well over forty hours per week). In return, companies provide, at best, minimal benefits, often leaving the employee responsible for the majority of costs and getting very little (if any) paid time off, among other things. If companies were to take better care of their employees, people would stay at their jobs and would be dedicated and loyal employees, resulting in broader support for American capitalism while destroying a major argument for socialism/communism.

---

19 The popular bumper sticker with the phrase "Coexist" is an example of how many Americans knowingly or unknowingly live according to Marxist principles.

There are necessary conditions for a successful battle to overthrow capitalism and for global liberation from various forms of oppression. Significant factors in achieving this grandiose victory include revolution and the unification of average workers and otherwise disenfranchised people from various countries and nations against the bourgeoisie of all countries and nations, because the main goal of the proletariat of all countries is global communism. This is the only reason communist and social democracies exist and why it must be understood that communism is a global movement that is constantly evolving. By virtue of this goal, the primary struggle and organization of average workers is internationalism. Internationalism is essentially an ideology that spreads friendships and partnerships between nations, international organizations (illegal and legal), and so on.[20]

Essentially, any communist party is a militant-revolutionary organization, including the Communist Party USA (CPUSA), which endorses the US Democratic Party. Communist parties and their front organizations are very well versed in how to operate underground and to do so by legitimate means, often taking advantage of freedom in any given nation (including the United States). Essentially, the totalitarian system of Russia is a unique blend of M-L and Asiatic despotism acquired when Russia was part of the Mongolian Empire. This idea is key to understanding Russia and its role in the modern global community. Remember that the Communist Party in Russia operated underground for decades before seizing power; it did so first with peaceful protests that culminated in violent uprisings against government representatives including the police. Therefore, the United States needs to pay close attention to the sociopolitical and economic dynamics occurring right now within this nation.

---

20 Internationalism is best spread by emphasizing the value of cultural diversity. Americans must understand that the communist concept of cultural diversity and associated legislation is currently being exploited through the fact that America is a nation of immigrants. Since the dissolution of the USSR, this concept has been increasingly widespread. Cultural diversity is intended to unite all peoples into one collective—one of the goals of communism.

The victory of the Great October Socialist Revolution in 1917 (which actually occurred in November on the Western calendar) established the world's first socialist multinational state, thus marking the beginning of a new historical epoch in the development of mankind. After Lenin passed away in 1924, the CPSU, together with its brother communist parties, continued to develop M-L theory. Based on Lenin's position and the creative application and development of the theory, the CPSU managed to build a communist society in the USSR. The CPSU worked out issues related to the possibilities of constructing socialism in a country located in a capitalist environment; the path, tempo, and means of socialist industrialization; the methods and forms of the collectivization of agriculture; and the path and means of conducting a sociological experiment known as a "cultural revolution." This is precisely why Americans need to take the time to study cultural Marxism, since it is the core aspect of the political correctness that has infected American society.

M-L serves as the international basis of revolutionary strategy and tactics for communist and workers' parties and the global solidarity of soldiers and militants for the cause of *all* oppressed classes—not just the working classes. Classic M-L takes into account specific historical features and the uniqueness of the circumstances in which every workers' party must operate; it always advocates the unity of international tactics for the communist movement. Proceeding from Lenin's previously stated position and the International Meeting of Communist and Workers' Parties (IMCWP) of 1960 and 1969, as well as the Non-Aligned Movement (NAM) established in 1961, it should be noted that the application of common laws for the development of socialist revolutions, socialist construction, and socialism in general should be achieved by taking into consideration the cultural-historical uniqueness of each country in the interest of the global socialist system on the whole.

The most important task for the CPSU and its brother communist parties throughout the world is the battle for the purity of M-L theory. The Cheka is responsible for this purification process, and this is precisely the core element of Chekism and is why all aspects of society need to be controlled. Experience has proven that modern revolutionary struggles and the strength of the global communist and socialist movements lie in the unwavering allegiance to M-L and the concept of internationalism in all spheres of society and life. Throughout its history, the CPSU has led the battle against all opponents of M-L. The IMCWP in June of 1969 reiterated and emphasized the necessity to strive for the triumph of M-L by utilizing creative and indecipherable methods in accordance with Lenin's directives of creative Leninism in achieving the victory of socialism and communism.

Lenin would be proud that his international revolution is evolving on a global scale, one country at a time, regardless of cultural or religious affiliation/orientation. In fact, Marxism-Leninism is becoming the new norm in the United States. Again, Americans are actively promoting Marxism-Leninism and do not even realize it via a variety of leftist movements and orientations. As a nation, we have been led to believe that the Soviet threat of global communism is history and that despite rocky relations, Russia (and even China and the Muslim world) are sometimes considered our allies in the global community despite being increasingly anti-American. For example, some of the major tenets of M-L encourage the advancement and protection of civil and human rights (including the right to quality education and to health care that is free or affordable), fair wages and workers' rights, feminism/women's rights and gender equality, environmental protection, equal distribution of wealth, gun control, democracy, animal rights, cultural diversity, ethics, peaceful coexistence, equal opportunity, nondiscrimination based on race and/or ethnicity, and especially the proliferation of social justice. M-L promotes these aspects to the maximum possible degree in the United States via the CPUSA, which advances its agenda via the US Democratic Party.

Together with colleagues from the special services of "former" communist countries, the Cheka engineered the fundamental issues and conditions necessary to develop a world socialist government. It utilized the concept of global governance through organizations, since organizations play an increasingly influential role in modern global society by unifying people and causes. This statement cannot be repeated enough. Chekists then researched the dynamics of modern capitalism in a postcolonial world and facilitated the necessary conditions to spread international revolutionary liberation and social movements on a global scale. This process continues to this day. An important takeaway in understanding M-L is that it maintains the argument that capitalism and capitalists cannot be reformed and therefore must be destroyed by any and all means necessary.

Chekism as a school of thought was perfected by Lavrentiy Beria, Aleksandr Sakharovsky, Yuri Andropov, and Yuri Drozdov of the KGB. This perception is uniquely rooted in Russia's thousand-year history and was born during the time when Russia was part of the Mongolian Empire, when its leaders adopted Sun Tzu's *Art of War* doctrine; the school of thought gained momentum during the Soviet period and now, in the post-Soviet period, is being perfected. Essentially, Putin's accession to the throne (so to speak) is symbolic of this dynamic. The security and intelligence services, colloquially known as the special services (*spets sluzhbi* in Russian), control all aspects and processes of Russian society. The major levers of societal control (and international control as well) include government and ideology, the military, the intelligentsia/Russian Academy of Sciences, the activities and operations of transnational terrorist organizations engaged in opposing the United States and the West in general, the activities and operations of transnational criminal networks, the cyberworld, and financial industries. Any type of "normal" political parties, dissident movements, public polls, the isolation of Russia, the existence of American-style government structures, and so on are strictly for show and controlled by the Chekists, since perception is a significant element of deception.[21] All of the organizations that Russia leads, is a member of, or is an observer of are control mechanisms to ensure that the goals of the Chekists are achieved.

Chekism considers terrorism to be more than just a strategy and tactic of maintaining the constant condition of revolutionary warfare; it is also a necessity designed to maintain its legitimacy, power, and control over

---

21 Golitsyn, 1995, p. 56.

society through a highly active leadership collective that operates behind the scenes. Chekists are also skilled with what they purport to be peaceful approaches that are centered upon the principle of socialism with a human face.[22] Dr. Ezepchuk informed me that the most aggressive Chekists often were also the strongest advocates of human rights. In this regard, it is interesting to point out that Pacepa and Rychlak argue that PLO chief Yasser Arafat, whom some believe to be a KGB creation, won the Nobel Peace Prize.[23]

State-supported terrorism and technological terrorism, the latter of which includes WMD programs, are essential tools of modern totalitarian political systems, and Russia is obviously no exception. Today, revolutionary terrorism takes many forms, including cultural revolutions and warfare, criminal radicalism, social movements, and protests. Social movements and protests obviously do not require the same response as a mass shooting or bombing incident but nonetheless are indicative of communist revolutionary dynamics.

Correspondingly, each solution requires a specific method of application to eradicate the root cause and not just the manifestations that are inherent to the reactionary "Band-Aid" approach. The method that is applied in response must be adequate, because inadequate and/or incorrect responses can exacerbate a situation.

A prime example of this is the US global war on terror. Rather than eradicating terrorism, America has created more terrorism through inadequate and inaccurate assessments of root causes and the true essence of the sources of threats. The small victories include thwarted terror attacks, but unfortunately these alone do not eliminate this cold warfare tactic. Therefore, at a minimum, an elementary comprehension of a situation/threat must be achieved. If not—and in accordance with the laws of nature—something else will replace the problem so that there will be no vacuum. Unfortunately, this concept creates confusion among American experts on terrorism and is precisely why once one terror

---

22 Dr. Ezepchuk interviews, 2015–2016.
23 Pacepa and Rychlak, Disinformation, p. 289.

organization appears to have been neutralized, another one will emerge to take its place. Giving terrorist organizations constant media attention does not help.

To reiterate, it is absolutely essential to understand that Islamic terrorism and other Islamic movements today are rooted in the Iranian Revolution of 1979, which itself was a manifestation of the Russian Revolution of 1917. Via the Tudeh Party and the KGB, a successful revolution was conducted in Iran, resulting in a totalitarian regime coming to power that actively supports terrorism both domestically and internationally and supports an extensive WMD program. Even the organizational structure, ideology, and tactics of the Hezbollah movement and the Iranian Revolutionary Guard Corps, including the Quds Force and Basij, provide evidence of the effectiveness of the KGB-FSB strategy in utilizing both peaceful and violent tactics, since they are products and partners of the Russian special services.

Although it is widely accepted that Alexander Yakovlev and Mikhail Gorbachev were the authors of *perestroika*, this historical event was actually developed within the depths of the Lubyanka (i.e., KGB headquarters). The deceptive seizure of the Russian leadership during the 1991 coup was the formulation of a multifaceted situation. Essentially, the KGB mafia took over Russia in the early 1990s, but before this world-changing event could take place, the world had to believe that global communism and the Soviet Union had failed. This is where *perestroika* came into play. In order to maintain control of the people, the security and intelligence services needed to develop an idea for the people—for example, that average Russian citizens desired an American type of democracy. But in reality this concept was false from the very beginning.

In terms of Russian leadership, it makes no difference whatsoever who sits in the Kremlin and what alleged party affiliation they have. Political parties are completely irrelevant aspects and distractions that are designed to keep American analysts offtrack—especially those who study individual leaders, political parties, and the intentions of both. What is important is achieving goals, such as exporting natural resources to as many points of the globe as possible—especially the West. Securing access to and the transport and control of natural resources is a critical element for the Cheka in maintaining power, control, and influence both domestically and internationally. These resources are not just oil and gas, as the media tends to focus on. Precious natural resources also include lithium,[24] diamonds, gold, silver, aluminum, copper, and water. The Eurasian continent—dominated by the special services of Russia and the former Soviet republics, Iran, and China—are in complete control of these resources. This competition for natural resources in Eurasia is the modern phase of the Great Game, which began in 1813 and continues to this day. Natural resources are at the core of the battle between Russia and the United States, including access to and control and transportation of the resources. Whatever nation controls these aspects essentially controls the overwhelming majority of the global flow of financial capital.

It makes no difference who is president or what a leader's party affiliation is, because it is the *spets sluzhbi* collective that is running the country. The American fetishization that focuses on individual leaders and their intentions (such as Putin, Assad, Kim Jong-un, and the like) as if they are acting alone and are not part of a collective leadership alliance is a fundamental mistake. The focus should instead be on cultural-historical processes and the role of the special services, socioeconomic and political dynamics of a target country, and the overarching mentality of that country. Since the United States is a relatively new and individualist society in comparison to Eurasian societies, this is a difficult concept for most Americans to comprehend.

Returning to *perestroika* and the August 1991 coup, the portrayal of a democratic image of people such as Mikhail Gorbachev, Yegor Gaidar, Grigory Yavlinsky, and Anatoly Chubais—all of whom are true, hardcore communists (colloquially called "social democrats," since the term "communism" is taboo in modern discourse)—was creatively utilized by the

---

24 Over $3 trillion worth of lithium are buried in the mountains of Afghanistan, where Russia, Iran, India, and China all have increasing influence. Also see http://www.telegraph.co.uk/news/worldnews/asia/afghanistan/7835657/Afghanistan-claims-mineral-wealth-is-worth-3trillion.html

Cheka (just as the Russian intelligentsia were); these people played their parts well. Soviet and post-Soviet Chekist leadership knew that American-style free-market capitalism and democracy would not work in the USSR. The territory of the former Soviet Union was too vast, both geographically and culturally, and M-L revolutionary ideology was (and continues to be) too deeply rooted in the minds of the people and leadership alike to be viable there.

In accordance with M-L, the strategy of revolutionary warfare and the various forms of terrorism are rooted in M-L; the strategy strives to alter the ideological positions of the population, thus resulting in confusion and a distorted perception of reality. This concept is based on the premise that a society is an artificially constructed organism that both evolves and can be easily altered and manipulated. Again, this is very easy to achieve in the United States, since very large portions of the population are more concerned about checking their Facebook pages, taking selfies, downloading the latest apps, prying into the lives of celebrities, drinking alcohol, doing drugs, and otherwise being too wrapped up in other distractions to take the time to become knowledgeable about the siege of America that is occurring right before our very eyes. The US homeland is under attack, yet millions of Americans remain stagnant in their individual microworlds.

Other dimensions of revolutionary terrorism (cold warfare/hybrid warfare tactics)[25] to achieve the goals of insurrectional warfare include propaganda, strategic disinformation, and psychological/information warfare. Today, many military experts are already in agreement that it is useless to defeat an enemy, and capturing territory is meaningless. The main goal is the task of establishing psychological control over the enemy's population, thus compelling the enemy to fulfill the will of the winner. This struggle is accomplished in a variety of ways when utilizing cold

---

25 Today, cold warfare tactics are addressed under the colloquial term "hybrid warfare." This approach to war that is utilized by Russia and its allies is nothing new; it gained momentum in the 1950s and has continued to evolve since the dissolution of the Soviet Union. The reason America is so focused on hybrid warfare now is because we have finally realized that traditional large-scale military operations are useless against an enemy that utilizes asymmetrical tactics as its primary doctrine.

warfare tactics. Contrary to popular opinion, the Cold War is not over. It merely transitioned into the final stage. Cold warfare tactics include the utilization of militant proxies, economic actions including sanctions and currency manipulation, information warfare/propaganda, espionage, legal warfare, transnational crime, cyberwarfare, attacks on the culture of a society, and political-military actions. None of these strategies and tactics ceased with the so-called end of the Cold War and dissolution of the USSR. In fact, they have expanded exponentially.

So what is a "cold war," exactly? According to my lecture notes from an international-security course I took in Moscow, a cold war is a prolonged state of conflict between nations that does not involve direct and traditional military actions/operations but is pursued primarily through economic warfare, including currency manipulation and protectionism, economic sanctions, political maneuvers, propaganda and information warfare, disinformation, waves of immigrant and refugee movements, espionage and cultural warfare operations, cyberwarfare, proxy warfare, and the proliferation of transnational crime. It is obvious that ever since the Cold War is supposed to have ended, these elements have not only persisted but have been exacerbated via the processes of globalization.

As previously mentioned, the Cold War transitioned into what Russia refers to as the "post-Soviet" stage. What better way to advance the goal of global Marxism-Leninism than to say that communism is dead and that the Soviet Union no longer exists while advancing communist ideology through different avenues and utilizing different and more peaceful and colloquial terminology? In contrast, China is an open M-L nation that is soon to become the world's leading economy; it holds billions of dollars of US debt, along with vast real-estate properties throughout the United States. Chinese people are paying cash for multimillion dollar mansions.

Large militaries are useless against the direct-action tactics of cold warfare. This form of decentralized and network-centered force is a promising military doctrine for enemies of the United States right here in the homeland—not just for our interests overseas. In this aspect, small but very technically well-equipped units independently operate over large areas and, if needed, are more than capable of performing a common task. In other words, such a doctrine is the theory of revolutionary warfare by insurgency or, more accurately, insurgency warfare.

The Cheka and Chekism utilize an elaborate schematic of decentralized organizational networks to achieve an aggressive, anti-American disposition, with each component playing a specific role in the overall system. In addition to illicit organizations, the FSB and the Foreign Intelligence Service (SVR) operate through their legitimate organizations, including the Commonwealth of Independent States (CIS); the Shanghai Cooperation Organization (SCO); the Organisation of Islamic Cooperation (OIC), an "observer" of the Non-Aligned Movement (NAM); the Collective Security Treaty Organization (CSTO); the International Congress of Industrialists and Entrepreneurs (ICIE), which previously operated as the Council for Mutual Economic Assistance; the World Peace Council, which is also an observer of the NAM; the International Progress Organization (IPO); the Organization of Solidarity with the People of Asia, Africa, and Latin America; the five industrialized powers known as the "BRICS" nations (Brazil, Russia, India, China, and South Africa); and the Alliance for Shared Values. These are the key organizations that the United States needs to be concerned with because they are extensions of the special services of America's most threatening enemies. These organizations are well structured and present rhetoric that is practically identical to that found in M-L.

Since the United States is the poster child of globalization and consumerism and accounts for an exceedingly large percentage of global consumption of goods and energy resources, the Russian special services believe that it is necessary for Americans to be restricted so that the whole world does not become Americanized and usurp the world's natural resources while straining societal infrastructural systems.

The Cheka also believes that the growth of the global population needs to be controlled to conserve natural resources and to minimize the strain on social and health-care systems as well as crucial natural resources such as oil, gas, and water. The sponsorship of terrorism, the facilitation of massive refugee migrations, the introduction of diseases to populations, the conducting of proxy wars, and the creation of WMDs are among the tools the Cheka utilizes to achieve these militant strategies of curbing global population growth. Dr. Ezepchuk also discusses how homosexuality is a natural occurrence that inhibits population growth. Also inherent to Chekism is the mentality that the fewer people there are, the fewer problems will exist.

The mafia leadership of the 1960s through 1980s, led by Khrushchev, Brezhnev, Andropov, and Gorbachev, despite advancing the idea of socialism with a human face, never had any intentions of establishing American-style democracy, because it is not suitable to the Russian/Soviet mentality. They cultivated and facilitated hate, especially toward the United States, which was strategically transferred to the third world. They did this so that people were pushed beyond their limits, to the point where they would demand iron fists and totalitarian rule.

In addition, according to the Hegelian dialectics inherent to M-L, society cannot progress without conflict, crisis, and instability. Therefore, these conditions must be created to achieve the desired outcome. This is animalistic in nature, but it is the truth. This dynamic is precisely what is occurring today in the United States.

Bolstering this school of thought, the ideology of Chekism is rooted in Indian fascism, because the Indian caste/pyramid system is the strictest and purest form of fascism.[26] In this system, people know their roles; if they are not managers, they do not try or dream of becoming managers. If they do, they will be met with harsh resistance and consequences. In addition, if people are perceived to pose any type of threat to the organs of the ruling elite, they are either discredited or destroyed.

The Cheka advises average citizens not to concern themselves with politics, because politics is considered a dirty business that is best left to the special services. This keeps the average citizen out of politics and from posing a threat to the government in general. It is important to

---

26 It is important to note that India was an ally of the Soviet Union and continues to be an ally of Russia today.

point out, however, that despite a lack of public participation in politics, the majority of Russians are well versed in politics. (At least that is what I observed from being immersed in Russian society for two years living with host families.)

After the dissolution of the USSR, the Cheka introduced privatization so that it would appear to be yielding to the Washington consensus, which, as noted earlier, was essentially a goal of the modern version of Lenin's New Economic Policy of the 1920s, which was to push Americans in the direction we wanted to go (completely unregulated capitalism) while attracting billions of dollars in business and financial investments from American corporations. Remember that history is of utmost importance to the Cheka. It portrayed privatization as a mechanism that allowed the average citizen to have ownership of and to profit from formerly state-controlled assets and industries so that everyone could enjoy the benefits of the allegedly accepted American-style capitalism. In reality, only the new Russians ("former" KGB personnel and high-ranking CPSU members and their families and friends) benefited from the alleged privatization process.[27]

This was just part of the plot to give *perestroika* a realistic appearance and to convey the notion that it was indeed viable in order to attract Western technology and financial support and investment; this also created opportunities for penetration by former communists of all aspects of American society, including leading academic institutions, think tanks, and government agencies. Furthermore, the breakup of the Communist bloc, giving "independence" to its various republics and nations, increases voting and representation in the United Nations.[28]

In order for the United States to counter the devastating effects on American domestic and foreign interests, we must admit that M-L and the Cold War did not just disappear when the Soviet Union ceased to exist as a geopolitical reality and subject of international law. Communist parties are prevalent and increasingly influential throughout the global

---

27 Essentially, privatization in the former Soviet Union was/is most recent version of state capitalism.

28 Please see Senate Intelligence Report link in appendix.

community, including right here in the United States of America. China is the best example, since it is becoming the economic leader of the world.

American political and economic leaders, along with American citizens in general, must therefore become familiar with communism, M-L, and Chekism in order to simplify their comprehension of modern global dynamics and the issues that affect everyone on the planet (whether they know it or not). Nearly everything that we are seeing around us is a direct result of a multitiered attack by our M-L enemies, who have convinced the world that communism died with the dissolution of the USSR and the alleged end of the Cold War. The reality is that the America that older generations knew and loved is being destroyed so that a pseudosociopolitical structure can take its place. It is time for America to take our country and culture back. As mentioned above, the first step is to study our enemies and to comprehend the number that the Russian special services and their allies are doing to us through the infiltration of our government, intelligence community, and a wide range of our institutions.

Therefore, Putin's Russia is a modern manifestation of the culmination of the successful construction of communism and the way in which Russia is controlled by the Russian special services; it is not a government with a president in charge of a state struggling to have an American-style democracy. Any information showing how Russia has a modern government structure, complete with political parties and representatives, is a complete farce that merely masks a totalitarian regime that is ruled and controlled by the Russian special services. Therefore, in developing an effective foreign policy toward Russia and its allies, we should not focus on opposition movements and similar distractions. The security and intelligence services in these countries are too deeply entrenched, and any opposition or pro-Western entity is a deception that needs to be ignored. There is no true "opposition" in these nations, because the average citizen has it ingrained in his or her consciousness to stay out of politics. Do not believe or trust anyone who says otherwise. Our foreign policy toward these nations needs to focus on their true intentions, which will be delineated in subsequent chapters of this book.

CHAPTER 5

Cold/Insurrectional Warfare

• • •

The following section is based on my notes from a lecture in Moscow in which I sat in on an entire three-hour class on Yevgeny Messner (a Russian military officer that helped develop the modern utilization of different aspects of insurrectional warfare) and insurgency/cold warfare tactics. Ever since the time when Russia was part of the Mongolian Empire (1240–1480), Russia's military doctrine has been centered upon Sun Tzu's Art of War *doctrine and has emphasized the use of asymmetrical tactics. Russia and China today do not hide their intentions of eliminating the United States as a global player in the international community. In addition to lecture notes, I also took notes while talking to an academic supervisor at this university, who informed me of the following.*

THE NEWEST STRATEGY OF ASYMMETRIC conquest has far-reaching consequences; it shows how those who plan and utilize terrorism realistically assess situations and evaluate the components of the modern global society. In a free democratic society such as the United States, there is an atmosphere of naïveté about global dynamics, thus making one of the primary goals of terrorism—instilling fear in order to disrupt the global political economy—relatively easy to do. The newest forms of terrorism are based on the fact that they consider asymmetry not as a temporary condition but rather as the key to long-term success. Winning is not their goal: prolonging the state of war and the condition of revolution to drain resources is their goal—just as has happened in Vietnam, Iraq, and Afghanistan. Unfortunately, American political and military leadership falls into this trap again and again.

Today, the latest forms of transnational terrorism are practically independent of the support of the local populations. The modern terrorist networks today that are working to destroy the traditional American way of life are much more dependent on infrastructural weaknesses (including the economic, physical, legal, and cultural aspects) of the United States while utilizing these vulnerabilities as weapons. This tactic makes it possible for weaker nations and organizations to compete with the United States on a level that favors America's enemies. At the same time, US leadership sends millions of dollars in financial aid to nations that are thought to be our partners yet are more aligned with Russia. Ukraine is one example. Although American democracy and our system of government are great for Americans, it is also the weakest form of government and the easiest in which to exploit weaknesses. Another contributing factor is that US political leadership is interested mainly in being elected and reelected and running the country from a corporate perspective. The United States is essentially becoming more like a large corporation with a weak, unstable foundation and less like a nation with a strong national defense.

Another issue is the current attacks on America's police and the trend of restricting them with legislation rather than working toward strengthening social and community responsibility. Glorifying criminal behavior while depicting law enforcement as uneducated racist pigs who abuse their power is a path to self-destruction. The converse needs to be the norm. Unfortunately, professional agitators, especially in groups such as Black Lives Matter, the New Black Panthers, the Nation of Islam, Occupy, and the media work together in riling people up against law enforcement, which could mean that communists are indeed in control of the media—one of the items of the Communist Goals Congressional Document from 1963 (listed in the appendix of this book).

After September 11, 2001, the United States launched the global war on terror (GWOT), and practically all civilized nations joined to fight in this struggle. Currently, the development of counterterrorism strategy, tactics, and plans for developing the armed forces is a major concern for the West. A major factor that is overlooked is that modern asymmetric warfare increasingly demonstrates characteristics of a strategy known as insurgency warfare. It is important to note that a key component of cold/insurgency warfare is to destroy the traditional cultural aspects of a society and to reshape its mentality at both the individual and societal levels. The conquering of the mind and soul is the modern field of battle. This is how America and Americans are currently under attack, and the battle against GWOT at this time needs to begin within our borders, not overseas.

Taking a glance at cold warfare operations, it has become noticeable to me that military allies have joined forces with the underground. For example, clandestine organizations, transnational criminal organizations, street gangs, and scattered networks of individuals, utilizing terrorism as an irregular warfare tactic, have developed a diverse range of motives, including (but not limited to) revenge against an occupier, the liberation of a people or nation, and sociopolitical upheaval. This mixture is compounded by the confusion of ideologies, which manifests itself in unprecedented forms of malice, protests, and riots.

Since the 1960s, insurgency and cold warfare tactics have been quite successful throughout the world. Its practitioners do not go by rules and use no recognizable templates: all aspects of a society are fair game. Cold warfare tactics are highly sophisticated forms of combat that are not comparable to classic, grand battles against large armies—an approach the US military continues to follow even though our enemies fight a different type of war. Simply throwing money toward large-scale conventional military operations at whatever is the perceived source of the threat will not solve this problem; this approach merely increases the effectiveness of cold warfare tactics and strategies while draining our resources.

Some of the cold warfare tactics that are applied on a regular basis include global revolutionary terrorism; transnational organized crime activities; uprisings; legal, political, and economic actions; and even protests and demonstrations. Within the United States, the last two components occur under the protection of the US Constitution. These tactics are known as direct action operations, which are inherent to Marxism. As discussed earlier in this book, Marxism came to Russia via the Russian intelligentsia. The intelligentsia provide the theoretical foundations of socialist revolution, which, according to Marxism, must be constantly maintained. This is why officers and agents from the Russian, Chinese, Iranian, African, Arab, and Cuban special services recruit people within educational systems, especially colleges and universities in the United States. Insurgency warfare operations occur in phases, including demoralization, riots, terrorism, the gradual recruitment of people into a revolution, and the restructuring of spiritual and even cultural principles. Restructuring cultural principles (by emphasizing cultural diversity as the strength of a nation) is precisely where the communist direct action operations of political correctness and legislation (an example of legal warfare) promoting cultural diversity come into play. Of course, affirmative action is another example of communist inspired legislation.

Unfortunately, societal agitators can exploit the First Amendment to begin revolutionary activity in this country and to pollute our educational system with the ideology of the Communist Party. The following chart is based on interviews I had with Dr. Ezepchuk and my contact in Moscow, as well as the 1963 "Goals of Communism" document link shown in the appendix.

Table 1: The destructive results of cold warfare operations and communist influences in the United States

Areas of Application and/or Infiltration	Strategies and Tactics	Current Manifestation
Religion	Discredit religion (primarily Protestant denominations); politicize, commercialize, and replace with cults; distract to other religions (Islam); work to get people disconnected from God to disempower individuals and society.	Lack of respect for humanity; atomization of society; death-wish mentality; feelings of despair; lack of hope and purpose. The proliferation of secular humanism.
American educational system	Shift focus from math, science, and foreign languages to gender/cultural studies; promote lower standards to minimize overall education levels; remove competition and make everyone a winner; spread the concept of political correctness.	Overall ignorance; reduced competiveness in global markets; overreliance on foreign workers in critical fields (engineering, IT, linguistics, etc.). Transformation of American educational system into a big business rather than being part of the foundation of national security

Areas of Application and/or Infiltration	Strategies and Tactics	Current Manifestation
Mass media	Gain control to psychologically manipulate the American people; stress nonissues and mass negativity rather than useful information; focus on violence, killing, and destruction to desensitize population to promote hopeless and negative mindset.	Widespread ignorance; distraction and attraction to nonsense to prevent understanding of issues. The media has power and influence over the population to dictate values, needs, etc.
Traditional American culture and values	Create false heroes and role models; glorify illicit behavior and the Sexual Revolution; politicize homosexuality; portray criminals as the good guys, oppressed and misunderstood by society; encourage negative image of police.	Widespread and increased addiction to drugs/alcohol and violent music, video games, and movies; idolization of celebrities/athletes, which desensitizes and corrupts the youth; lack of respect for public-service professionals such as police officers and teachers; increase in criminal activities.

Areas of Application and/or Infiltration	Strategies and Tactics	Current Manifestation
Law and order	Govern through legislative action while discarding moral principles; work to eliminate constitutional rights such as the Second Amendment; strive to legalize marijuana in all fifty states.	Lack of faith in an effective judicial system. Destabilization of society through social movements such as Black Lives Matter and Occupy Wall Street; increases in drug use to weaken the people.
Societal relations	Continue to promote individualism; rely on modern psychology and sociology based on the Frankfurt school / critical theory and emphasize the importance of political correctness.	Less individual sense of responsibility and decreased respect for others.
National security	Infiltrate fields of security, police, military, and intelligence.	Vulnerable population; placement of heritage/ native speakers of foreign languages in US national security and think-tank positions to help Americans interpret the role of Russia and its allies in the global community.

Areas of Application and/or Infiltration	Strategies and Tactics	Current Manifestation
Domestic politics	Influence and infiltrate both political parties and create conflicts between parties; politicize issues such as homosexuality and racism; strive for gun control to disarm Americans.	Disunity and division within and between political parties at the state/national levels; law-abiding citizens must confront criminals, who get guns regardless of laws.
Foreign policy	Partner with US allies; maximize the use of proxies such as terrorist organizations and transnational criminal organizations as a method of warfare; promote arms-reduction treaties; set up parallel economic/political system through organizations such as the SCO to eliminate the US role in global affairs; destroy the dollar to be replaced with the Russian ruble or the Chinese yuan; create artificial political crises to attract money from American leaders.	Isolation of the United States in the global community and the proliferation of anti-Americanism; destroyed national budget, resulting in economic crashes and a lack of finances to fund national defense; imminent elimination of the dollar as a global reserve currency.

Areas of Application and/or Infiltration	Strategies and Tactics	Current Manifestation
Family and society	Break up and destroy on as many levels as possible; create reliance on noneffective and bureaucratic social-services system. Promote divorce as normal and acceptable.	Societal tensions and disunity; destroyed concept of community; increased homelessness. Raising of children with no concept of the strengths of a nuclear family and/or acceptance of same sex parents.
Health of population	Seek to add synthetic ingredients to food; introduce more medications with side effects, thus creating other medical and psychological conditions; destroy the nation's health-care system.	Disabled masses due to health problems, diseases, and food allergies; strain on the national health-care system (both public and private); unaffordable health-care insurance.
Race	Lower the image of whites; advocate minority movements, rights, protests, riots, etc.	Hatred; societal divisions; unfair affirmative-action laws; reverse-discrimination.

Areas of Application and/or Infiltration	Strategies and Tactics	Current Manifestation
The American economy and the average worker*	Create conditions for class struggle and social stratification; infiltrate corporate America to take away workers' rights and continue to exploit workers despite legislation; keep wages low so majority of working class cannot keep up with inflation; support and continue to push the United States into more unregulated capitalism (i.e., neoliberalism.)	Massive unemployment and underemployment and the intensification of financial crises. Erosion and eventual elimination of the middle class, increased debt, especially student loans.

* The final item on this list later included the promotion of the Washington consensus, essentially pushing the United States in the direction that communists want.

The above evidence is precisely why communism is destructive to American society. When we ask ourselves what is going on with our nation, these areas are the core components of our situation. At the same time these revolutionary operations are taking place, Americans are guided toward the humanitarian issues that communists and socialists promote. Once the initial transformation phase is complete, the purified form of M-L, Chekism, will come into play, just as it did in every other communist country in the world. Socialism will then be introduced by force upon American society, and our freedom and independence will be gone forever.

CHAPTER 6

Dr. Ezepchuk on the Cheka

• • •

This chapter is concerned with the official substitution of the Communist Party's revolutionary power with that of the Chekists. This chapter is based on personal interviews with and material written by my friend and colleague Dr. Ezepchuk.

THE DISINTEGRATION OF THE SOVIET Union in 1991 and the coming of power of the supposedly healthy democratic forces of society revealed the true picture of the balance of political forces in the post-Soviet space. Nearly everything that was masked during the Soviet regime became evident after the USSR's demise.

After ten years in power, the democrats in Russia revealed an extremely important phenomenon: the merging of the will of the people and the Chekist organization. What guided the USSR was not the unity of the Communist Party and the people, as the leadership had declared for over seventy years, but rather the covert activities of the KGB organization. The KGB operated for decades in the shadows while it hid behind the leadership role of the Communist Party despite being interwoven into the heart and soul of the CPSU. It was the KGB that transformed the newly democratic Russia back into a police state. The Western-oriented democrats were pushed aside, and the Chekists officially came to the surface of political life; they demonstrated a high level of organizational structure, with strict discipline and cohesion of its ranks. More than half the Russian population including both the people and the Chekists claim they are expressing their aspirations. To this day, there is yet to be any type of official written description of how this repressive organization ascended to the Mount Olympus of Soviet politics. After the death of Stalin, however, Soviet premier Nikita Khrushchev and other Soviet strategists unofficially formulated a policy of thawing relations with the West and spread the policies of Leninism, which were based on peaceful coexistence. Khrushchev formulated his own personality cult and had extremely aggressive policies, strategies, and tactics against the United States and the Western world in general. The peaceful approaches were merely Lenin's tactics, which were proven effective during the New Economic Policy.

To promote the new policy of peace and to support the new role of the KGB in widening their operations to include a focus on the spread of global communism, the Soviets developed the slogan "Let us beat our swords into plowshares." This is a phrase based on Isaiah 2:2-4 that is a call to replace hostility with peace in order to live a productive life. This citation from the Bible was meant to deceive and appeal to the conservative American political leadership. The Soviet artist and sculptor Yevgeny Vuchetich even constructed a monument depicting this slogan in 1957–1959, which stands in the garden of the United Nations to this day. An associated communist slogan that continues to this day is, "Peace for life." Dr. Ezepchuk is convinced that knowing the history of the Cheka is the key to comprehending the true role of this organization in domestic and international events during both Soviet and post-Soviet times.

The Cheka was established by commissars in the initial years of Soviet leadership for the struggle against counterrevolutionaries as a continuation of the secret/political police of the Russian Empire. After the bolsheviks were victorious in the Russian Civil War, however, the struggle against counterrevolutionaries no longer posed an imminent threat. The task of reforming and educating the "irresponsible" and "thoughtless" elements of the new society in labor camps was added to the duties of the Cheka. As before, the Cheka maintained its punitive functions, but its activities became more focused on defending the victories of the Russian Revolution on a global scale.

When Stalin began his rise to power in 1924, the functions of the Cheka started to expand. This was preceded by a split in the ranks of the Communist Party that was artificially created by the fraudulent and deceptive policies of the Stalinist party leadership. The purpose of the split was to discredit the political authority of Trotsky, who was second in party ranking after Lenin, by declaring him the head of the interparty opposition. The next stage of the process was to formulate a plan to destroy the opposition, supposedly in the name of party unity and solidarity. Since that time, two primary responsibilities of the Chekists has been the struggle for the purification of the party ranks and the eradication of all dissent in the ranks—not only of the party but of the state in general. In essence, this purification process is yet another aspect of Chekism.

The innovative concept of creating false opposition was designed in order to expose those who presented a threat to the future plans of the new leadership. This concept is still applied today as an effective mechanism in identifying American or American-supported operatives conducting insurrectionary activities in foreign countries to overthrow pro-Russia governmental officials in order to replace them with pro-American governmental leadership. The seemingly pro-American leaders (who in reality are pro-Russian including Petro Poroshenko) are part of a greater plan to usurp the provision of financial assistance from the United States and to give American leadership false hope and a false sense of security that its strategies are working. In actuality, these pan-American strategies are doomed to failure and are a diversion of not only clandestine operations against American international interests abroad but also within the borders of the United States.

Returning to the initial development of this strategic phenomenon, the ranks of the opposition included not only thousands of party members but the majority of commissars, who were at the forefront of the bolshevik revolution. To accuse these figures of counterrevolutionary activities would be unlikely, as they were devoutly committed to the October revolution and demonstrated loyalty to the revolution on all fronts, which led to the end of the Civil War. The inventive minds of the leaders then expanded the arsenal of Chekist rhetoric by calling former colleagues in the party "enemies of the people." The Chekists subjected these enemies to total destruction. The extermination process dragged on for years. Tens of thousands of enemies of the people lost their lives, and for decades, millions of citizens were sent into exile or labor camps within the Soviet gulag system.

In 1997, a book titled *The Commissar Vanishes* by the British historian David King was published. This book discusses the massive destruction of the revolutionary party and the elimination of its leaders. King also shows how numerous photos were altered during the course of Soviet history: important revolutionary figures, members of the first Soviet government, and heroes of the Russian Civil War were erased from historical documents. The idea was to erase these alleged enemies of the state from the collective memory in order to support Stalinism.

From the battles with the enemies of the people, the Chekists emerged not only as victors: they gave themselves the right to command and control all aspects of life throughout the country. The party removed the remnants of revolutionary bolshevism and lost its political power. The party's declared leadership role was then assumed by the geniuses of all time and all peoples, which was based on and guided by the mighty army of security and intelligence officers. In other words, the Communist Party of the Soviet Union became the governing structure in conjunction with the Chekist organization. The Cheka is the military-political-police entity that is part of the CPSU.

The organization of security officers has come a long way over the decades from the destruction of the commissars and their associates. The organization has been careful to conceal these activities both at home and abroad. The name of the Chekist organization has repeatedly changed, as have the names and titles of its leaders, but its very essence is always left unchanged—the leaders of the CIS, who maintain constant control over the "independent" nations and all aspects of life of their peoples.

The political and commanding ambitions of the organization of security and intelligence officers expanded year by year until finally the

Chekist organization had turned into a mafia organization, which captured the main levers of power of the totalitarian regime, thus simultaneously combining the function of a political vanguard and punitive function. Stalin can be considered the creator of this model of political system, which was based on the history of Russian autocratic government models. After spreading the slogan "Cadres decide everything," Stalin shifted all personnel policy and politics to the Chekists, who zealously solved the problems of the selection and placement of people at all levels of government and party life. This is precisely how Russia became an intelligence-police state today that maintains its influence over all of the member nations of the CIS and throughout the world.

After developing the passport-registration system of the population, which involved completing background-security forms, the Chekists got their hands on detailed information about every person living in the territory of the USSR. This system is still in place throughout the CIS and even includes foreigners, including students such as myself. I remember completing an abbreviated version of this form each time I went to Russia; it included such questions as current/recent employment, information on immediate family members, education, experience if any with firearms, and so on. By ending the existence of the USSR and improving diplomatic ties with the United States, Russia was able to gain access to information on Western citizens who travel to Russia. At the same time, KGB agents and officers could freely travel to the United States as businessmen seeking to pursue the American dream. This was an ingenious plan to infiltrate American society at all levels that has assisted in hiring sons and daughters of KGB agents into positions with national security responsibilities throughout the US government and intelligence community.

The USSR was covered by a network of the First Department (foreign intelligence) of the KGB. This department was the largest and most pervasive of the KGB and is today known as the SVR. The First Department managed data on the social background, occupation, and reliability of every citizen. The simultaneous introduction of this so-called regime of registration provided the opportunity for the Cheka to control people and their places of residence. This function of selection of the KGB-FSB-SVR continues to be very valued, because it allows the entire population to be subordinate to the security and intelligence services—including party leadership.

All governmental aspects of the registration forms were controlled by the Chekists. They gave (and continue to give) commands on who is reliable and who is not and ultimately who to get rid of by discrediting or assassinating. The Chekists determine who gets into what schools and when, as long as the student is not Jewish. Ever since the early days of the Soviet Union, Russia has maintained an anti-Zionist state policy both domestically and internationally. An indirect manifestation of this policy is the regime's support from the entire Muslim world.

As with the snowball effect, the number of secret bases and organizations that are ruled by the KGB-FSB continues to increase; the KGB-FSB was granted the right to determine what should be considered classified and those aspects of life that require special modes of operation.[29]

Cheka chief Lavrentiy Beria headed the project of creating a special construction bureau that was designed for enriching nuclear materials and creating atomic weapons. All geological activities associated with the development of uranium deposits (development in which most of the labor force were prisoners) was controlled by the security services. Even with the demise of the Soviet Union, the Cheka maintained tight security and control over these destructive weapons. Today, Russia supports Iran's nuclear program and even conducts uranium enrichment for Iran within the borders of the Russian Federation to deceive Western inspectors.

The pitiful remnants of religious cults that had been allowed by the Soviets were also under the heels of the Chekists. According to Dr. Ezepchuk, evidence was discovered in the archival materials that the future head of the Russian Orthodox Church was recruited by the security services.

---

29 Based on Dr. Ezepchuk's firsthand experience, back in the 1940s, the entire field of atomic energy was placed under the control of the Chekists, who were in control of the Ministry of Defense.

By utilizing deception and lies, the guardians of the regime destroyed the logic of healthy thinking and aroused in the people suspicion and hostility toward one another. Lying was the primary method that the security services used to destroy the psyche of the people. Similar dynamics are occurring right here in America. Furthermore, if the Chekists regularly lie and deceive their own people, it is foolish to think that the KGB was telling us the truth about the collapse of the Soviet Union and the numerous shortcomings and failures of communism.

The Marquis de Custine, who visited Russia in the nineteenth century, made an interesting observation. He wrote, "In Russia to lie means to retain the throne, while speaking the truth means to shake the foundations of the State."[30] This striking feature of the mentality of the Russian people, noticed a hundred years ago, was put to service by the *oprichniki* (a version of the KGB established by Ivan the Terrible in 1565) of the new Soviet regime.

For over thirty years, while the government tyrant (Stalin) created a police state remained in power, the Cheka organization became an integral component of the ruling elite. The Chekists valiantly guarded the myth of the genius of the leadership and the mystery of betrayal of their fellow members of the Bolshevik Party, along with the bloody crackdown on those party members.

Khrushchev lifted the veil that covered the evil and tyranny that prevailed in the country, in which millions of Soviet citizens were victims. By focusing all attention on the cult of personality and removing Beria and a few of the leading security officers around him, Khrushchev decided that the repressive machine had been stopped and believed that the danger of a return to the past no longer existed. Having spent a lifetime in the leadership of the party, he did not notice that the political police of the Cheka had become the main force governing the country and firmly held the levers of power in their grasp.

The Chekists had long grown out of the youthful leather jackets they'd worn in the early days when executing counterrevolutionaries. Having

---

30 De Custine, Marquis. Empire of the Czar: A Journey Through Eternal Russia (1839)

grown up in the struggle with the commissars dressed in the uniforms of the sinister Stalinist cut, they had forever changed the philosophy of revolutionary romanticism while abusing the people. Very soon the Chekists were reminded of the short-sighted reforms that need to be considered. The days of Khrushchev's rule were numbered.

Having gained vast experience in the field of the selection and placement of personnel, security officers found a suitable candidate and easily managed general who valued their services to the motherland. The time of Leonid Brezhnev's reign became the golden age for the Chekists. The ranks of the security and intelligence services were supplemented by thousands of graduates of universities and academies of different specialties; their great helmsman, dethroned by Khrushchev, was almost completely rehabilitated, their organizational structure was renewed, and the political influence on state governance and in international affairs rose to unprecedented proportions.

Those who called the rule of Brezhnev a time of stagnation were correct; indeed, the absence of progressive social reforms provides grounds for this point of view. But the reforms of Brezhnev's politburo—hidden from the eyes of the public—were strengthening the security and intelligence services. This strengthening of the security services also included increasing their role in international affairs politically, economically, culturally, socially, militarily, criminally, and clandestinely. A primary conduit for such operations was (and still is) the United Nations and the numerous international organizations that promote social justice and anti-imperialism.

Under Brezhnev, the KGB was given control over the entire diplomatic community (including the Ministry of Foreign Affairs, which is the primary diplomatic arm of the FSB and SVR today), took control of key functions of the state, and merged the political, economic, social, and cultural spheres with the criminal spheres in order to ensure complete control over all aspects of life in the USSR. The KGB transformed the Soviet Union into the largest and most highly staffed mafia corporation in the world. A new ruling elite began to form that sought to obtain a different kind of wealth through corporate connections (both legal and illegal). This group became known as the *blat*.[31]

Awards, degrees, and important titles became fashionable in the Brezhnev era. The elite surrounded itself with a network of private clubs, salons, hospitals, health spas/resorts, and recreation centers that were only available to themselves and their family and friends; within elite universities, promising graduates were guaranteed work abroad. These special privileges were only given to the offspring of those who had connections with the Chekist organization. For these special individuals, the path to an enriching life existed beyond the borders of the homeland.

Having opened loopholes in the Iron Curtain, the Chekists used any means necessary to experience travel abroad for any number of reasons. The Chekists included themselves in tourist and scientific groups, various delegations and missions traveling abroad, international organizations, representative governmental offices, and embassies. Security and intelligence officers were scattered all over the world in search of personal enrichment while at the same time carrying out assignments of the Chekist organization and as dictated by the objectives of the Cold War.

Membership in the Chekist organization gradually became a profitable business. In the homeland, where the purchase of any household items had turned into an unsolvable problem (due to shortages, long lines, etc.), those who returned from business trips abroad were able to improve their overall quality of life in alignment with Western standards. Foreign gifts were very much appreciated in their native land and were successfully used for winning promotions and even in obtaining scientific degrees.

Dr. Ezepchuk recalls one instance in which an employee who worked in the World Health Organization returned to Moscow with the desire to become a doctor of science; he quickly found employment at the Gamaleya Institute, where Dr. Ezepchuk was based. Despite having weak skills in

---

31 Blat is a slang word from the criminal underground society (formed within the gulag system) that can signify connections, influence, and/or protection. This term also represents how Russians circumvent laws and rules by payoffs, threats, blackmail, extortion, and intimidation. Essentially, it is a phenomenon of Russian cultural history that manifested during the Soviet period and continues to this day.

academic and scientific research, in just two years he had defended his thesis, which he completed at the level of an undergraduate student. But since the graduate had gained the support of the thesis director and the scientific department, his work had passed all the necessary steps. Soon afterward, he had a doctorate of science and had begun a career as a business entrepreneur.

During the Brezhnev era, corruption and the degradation of morals became a universal phenomenon. The harsh slogan of the bolsheviks, "He who does not work shall not eat," had turned into its opposite by the seventh decade of Soviet power. The consumer demands of the new ruling elite—who did not create any material or spiritual wealth—did not compare with the pathetic way of life for the average working citizen, whose primary source of subsistence was farming or in some type of manufacturing. "Sausage for the people," as the arrogant ruling elite proclaimed, was the luxury food item that was distributed among the common people. The people did not complain, however, and were comforted by the thought that conditions had been far worse during the Second World War.

Indeed, the patience of the Russian people is infinite. A Russian is ready at any moment to sacrifice himself in the name of faith, whether it is faith in God, faith in the tsar, or faith in Stalin and Putin. The Russian man never belongs to himself because he is always ready to sacrifice his life for his family, clan, and homeland. The mind of the Russian man has always been enslaved, and he has never valued his individual life as much as that of the collective. He sees himself as part of a lordly order that he belongs in.

The Soviet power turned Russian men into *lumpen* and used all forces possible to deprive the individual of a beginning and to create a social being. At the same time, Soviet leadership also transformed Russia from a state of serfdom into a leading global society representing the progressiveness of all humanity.

The predictions of the Russian intellectuals of the nineteenth century foretelling the "universal mission" of the *Russian Idea* did not come true. Instead, from the depths of the Russian mentality came the ominous specter of the KGB that threatened the entire world with terror and violence. At its inception, the KGB declared itself a terrorist organization. To this day, the KGB/FSB/SVR is the epitome of all transnational terrorist organizations. In formulating US foreign policy on Russia, this fact needs to be considered.

Russia's historical experience has shown that the transplantation of culture of one civilization onto the national soil of another is a painful process. As in medicine, very often a transplant is accompanied by symptoms of rejection and interference from the body of the recipient. While modern clinical science has found ways to resist transplant rejection in the recipient, the transplantation of human society is another matter. The effectiveness of any transplantation of society must stand the test of time. This is what is happening in the United States as liberals (communists) continue to gradually transform America into a communist state.

Modern Russia continues to be tormented by an inferiority complex that has existed among its people from the time of Peter the Great's reforms, which put Russia on the European track of development. This complex was overcome by the elite of the nation; this elite once comprised the nobility but was scattered throughout the world after the bolshevik revolution. The part that remained in Russian territory declared itself the creator of a new culture. This new culture was not enriched with the spiritual life of humanity and gave nothing to the world except the Kalashnikov assault rifle (which may be found in the hands of virtually every terrorist) and the creation of some the world's most prolific terrorist organizations, such as the PLO, the Army of the Guardians of the Islamic Revolution/Iranian Revolutionary Guard Corps (including the Quds Force and Basij), Hamas, FARC (the Revolutionary Armed Forces of Colombia), and Hezbollah.

All of these dynamics take place against the backdrop of a reignited arms race and other forms of chemical, nuclear, radiological, and biological warfare (Russia refers to these operations as "technological terrorism"), drawing on the knowledge of the scientific community and the Russian intelligentsia in general. Unfortunately, the Russian intelligentsia has no choice but to comply and continue with the ongoing process of the militarization of science. Because of this, scientists are given tremendous trust and responsibility while at the same time having their morals and ethics challenged daily. In order to verify loyalty, the special services constantly place scientists in positions in which they have to defend, explain, and justify their actions. Finally, due to the nature of the scientific community in Russia being controlled by the Cheka, all fields of science and the humanities are therefore inextricably linked to politics and cannot be effectively analyzed individually.[32]

---

32 Dr. Ezepchuk interviews, 2015–2016.

Conclusion/Investigative Summary

• • •

REVOLUTIONARY TERRORISM TAKES MANY FORMS other than bombings; it contributes to both the annihilation of society and individuals, particularly at the local level, which most people overlook and/or underestimate. Other forms of revolutionary terrorism include drug sales/trafficking and drug cartels, the illegal activities of street gangs, human trafficking, the limiting of access to healthy organic food to the wealthy, the proliferation of disease epidemics introduced into populations by the Russian special services and/or their allies, the artificial creation of economic crises, cultural warfare, the manipulation of religion,[33] the facilitation of satanic cults, criminal radicalism, instrumental Marxism, totalitarian religious sects, the degeneration of the US educational system, homosexual propaganda, antipolice movements and protests, the gun control movement, the proliferation of pornography and prostitution, and so forth. Not only are these activities morally corrupt but they cloud the consciousness with crippling mind-sets and behavior and, worse, are so common that films and books promote them as intriguing points of view. In addition to terrorist attacks, these are the primary forms of terrorism (cold warfare tactics) to affect US national security.

---

33 This is done by perverting religions such as Christianity, Islam, and Judaism to facilitate radicalism and violence, neither of which is an actual element of these religions.

The American reader knows much more about the essence of fascism (under Nazi Germany) than the essence of the totalitarian regime (under the USSR) and even less about the USSR's inheritor—the Commonwealth of Independent States. Details about the lives of average people who lived behind the Iron Curtain have gone virtually unnoticed in comparison to the lives of Western Europeans during World War II. This is a great tragedy, as the West is missing many pieces to the puzzle of an entire period of Russia's cultural history known as the Soviet period of Russian history.[34]

Without having complete comprehension of the dynamics inherent to Soviet society, America will not be able to effectively deal with Russia in any and all aspects of global affairs. In fact, these very dynamics that occurred during the Soviet period have led to the ascent of Putin's junta, which has resulted in the destruction of Russia's attempt at becoming a Western-style capitalist democracy. This presents a major threat to the entire civilized world.

The prediction of the human-rights activist Yelena Bonner (wife of the former Soviet nuclear physicist and later dissident Andrei Sakharov, both of whom were friends of Dr. Ezepchuk and his wife Sonia) has come true. She stated that appointing a KGB officer head of the Russian government after the dissolution of the USSR is similar to appointing a gestapo officer as the leader of Germany after the defeat of fascism.[35]

Stalin betrayed the bolsheviks and created a socioeconomic, political, and cultural system that to this day is completely under the control of the Chekists. The Chekists initially provided cover for crimes that were committed by the Stalin regime. The Chekists then created a network of concentration camps known as gulags to isolate and physically destroy the enemies of the people, which created an impetus for Russian organized crime to develop. The Iron Curtain hid these crimes against humanity and inhibited the spreading of any information that would educate the rest of the world on these dynamics—dynamics that are unprecedented

---

34 Езепчук, Ю.В. 2010. Одна жизнь на двух континентах. Москва: Новый Хронограф.
35 Ibid.

at the global scale and yet another major obstacle to truly comprehending Russian domestic and foreign policy today.

The Chekists have been and continue to be in charge of Russian domestic and international relations. Their main methods to maintain legitimacy, power, and control include terror, lies, and deception. Chekists effectively suppress any form of protest, and any protests that take place in the former Soviet Union are implemented and supervised by undercover KGB-FSB officers who work with unsuspecting American political and academic entities and personnel that are attempting to align former Soviet republics with the United States. Americans cannot seem to comprehend the fact that all of the former Soviet republics are inextricably connected by the special services of these countries, including Ukraine and the Baltic states, who continue to work very closely together despite rhetoric (propaganda) stating the contrary. The Chekists filter, control, and produce all media and information outlets and destroy all who pose any type of threat: either by killing them or by slandering them to the point that they are discredited and can no longer play a role in educating the global community about their operations.

Throughout the over-seventy-year Soviet period of Russian history, a new population of people was created—the Soviet people—also known by the term *Homo sovieticus* mentioned earlier. In the modern global community, particularly in America, a cultural transition has been taking place in which an American version of *Homo sovieticus* is being created. The social system created by Stalin with the help of the KGB utilized elements of Christianity to create a secular moral code that controlled the entire consciousness of the population regardless of previous religious affiliation. Masters in this area of operations graduated from special, top-secret university programs that taught how to present lies as virtual truth and how to skillfully replace truth with lies. They reduced civilized morality and ethics; they were (and still are) bound by the monolithic belief in the persistent existence of a hostile environment.[36]

---

36 Dr. Ezepchuk interviews, 2015–2016.

The imperialistic ambitions of modern Russia have been revived—along with a renaissance of Marxist-Leninist ideology and religious messianism—that together render the world a breeding ground for terrorism and transnational crime, regionalism, nationalism, and xenophobia in conjunction with the evolution of a totalitarian state that is focused on the role, power, and control of the security and intelligence services over the population as well as the global community as a whole.

Therefore, Chekists perceive the surrounding world as a constant enemy. Propaganda maintains this disposition. The propaganda of the current Putin junta has the same purpose that it had under the Soviet regime: to enlist the support of the unthinking masses in the junta's criminal actions.[37]

The Soviet Union developed an extensive program of assistance to the developing nations of the third world, including Africa, Latin America, and the Islamic world. In doing so, in accordance with Marxism-Leninism and the advancement of the communist revolution (which is a continuous global movement that takes many diverse forms to this day), these nations were used to advance the struggle for liberation of the people from capitalist oppression, colonialism, and exploitation. The KGB officers in these countries educated and trained many elements of these societies in how to utilize terrorism and a diverse range of civil, social, racial, cultural, and political movements to achieve liberation from various forms of Western influence. These movements began to manifest in the United States beginning in the 1960s and continue to this day. Today, numerous terrorist organizations, including IS/ISIS, Hezbollah, and the Iranian Revolutionary Guard Corps, among others, successfully and widely use the arsenal of these methods to achieve their criminal goals. These insurrectionary operations of the FSB and SVR and their allies continue to manifest all over the world today, especially in the United States.

Today, Putin's junta and the Russian Special Services are in the process of constructing a hybrid of the Mongolian Empire, the Russian Empire, and the USSR. Without truly comprehending all aspects of Russian

---

37 Ibid.

history, particularly Soviet history, the United States will be ineffective in dealing with the diverse range of threats that are posed by Russia and its numerous allies. Russia has already launched a new global arms race, only this time the WMDs are much more advanced (although they are still firmly rooted in Soviet science, particularly of the 1950s to 1970s).

Since the Russian Revolution of 1917, the Chekists have been the sole creators of political ideology. Putin and the overwhelming majority of leaders from the CIS are products of the KGB system and are continuing to use the same methods of operation, including disinformation (operations of planting lies and deception) through repressive measures, assassinations, slander, and falsification.

One of the greatest tactics developed by the KGB was to utilize radical Islam to advance the global communist revolution. This strategic maneuver was first conceptualized prior to the bolsheviks coming to power through the manipulation of Islam and Muslims in the Soviet Union beginning in the early 1900s; this strategy was first implemented in the 1960s and is still highly effective against the United States. It is literally chipping away at the overall defense capability of our nation due to the tremendous financial and human resources used to combat this pervasive threat. This book is more than a personal narrative on global revolutionary terrorism, the Russian system of state security, and Putin's junta. It is a tool to assist Americans in comprehending and dealing with the wide range of issues facing the world today.

Ultimately, ideology fomenting revolutionary mind-sets is destructive, reactionary, and harmful for the everyday lives of American citizens. Revolutionary ideology is formulated on a foundation of lies and severely twisted philosophical points of view. The revolutionary ideology inherent to Marxism-Leninism and Chekism is not only destructive but also reactionary to the point that it arouses and drives individuals, groups of people, organizations, and even some governments to commit the most unfathomably barbaric acts using increasingly horrific means of homicide, assassination, and genocide, all rooted in the social theoretical philosophy of antihumanism. Undertaking the in-depth study of Marxism-Leninism is the key to understanding this unfortunate phenomenon. The best representative platforms of revolutionary ideology are rooted in a) aggressive and reactionary nationalism, b) ersatz and distorted religious perceptions, c) eschatological perceptions, d) extremism, e) radical criminology, and f) instrumental Marxism and Marxism-Leninism in general.[38] It is crucial that American experts analyze these topics in order to more effectively advance the GWOT.

The best strategies to begin to save the United States include a spiritual revival[39] and the education of Americans about Marxism-Leninism, the role of the CPUSA (along with its partner communist parties and organizations throughout the world), and the process of cultural warfare that is performed under the cover of "peace." The last Christian revival in the United States occurred in the early 1900s. Christianity must be revived in the United States, because these principles are what our nation was founded upon. Christianity is a crucial aspect of American society because it is the pillar of our spiritual and moral principles: it raises the value of all people, gives people creative energy, serves society with ideas of creation (rather than destruction), and unites rather than divides people. Ultimately, Americans' faith in God must be restored. If the American media were no longer under the control of communists, then there would no longer be a reason not to endorse TV shows, movies, and news that strive to promote peace, justice, beauty, family values, social responsibility, and love rather than hate, graphic violence, torture, and murder.[40] This will not be an easy process thanks to the cultural degradation led by Russia and its allies and sympathizers that has infiltrated and destroyed traditional American values over two generations and counting.

---

38 Dr. Ezepchuk interviews, 2015–2016.

39 A spiritual revival would occur through a return to the traditional Christian values our nation was founded upon through the positive promotion of the role of the church in American society and by living according to the Bible rather than by secular humanistic ideals and philosophies imposed upon us by the communists.

40 The radio station K-Love is an excellent source for promoting Christian values and positive aspects of life in connection to God. This radio station could potentially serve as a type of launching platform for a Christian spiritual revival in the United States.

Despite popular discourse, communism and Chekist concepts of revolution have not disappeared but rather have evolved into different forms that are so unrecognizable that they have become unnoticeable and acceptable to Americans. World War III is definitely underway: the main field of battle is the mind, using a system of psychology rooted in cold/hybrid warfare. In these types of operations, there are no boundaries or rules; every person and culture throughout the world is a target, including women and children. Of course, making the national security of the United States more of a priority than foreign pursuits is paramount; this includes stopping the giving of billions of dollars away to countries that turn around and align themselves more with Russia and China than with the United States. Simply throwing money at various programs regardless of their effectiveness and without a comprehensive understanding of the true dynamics of global revolutionary terrorism and all its aspects is a misguided approach that is doomed to failure.

Finally, in Moscow in 2013, my Russian colleague warned me that Hillary Clinton will succeed Barack Hussein Obama as president of the United States, thus facilitating and finalizing the process of bringing America under the sphere of influence of Russia and China officially by May 9, 2020—Russia's Victory Day. Therefore, it would be wise for all Americans to learn either Russian or Mandarin Chinese. Only time will tell, but there is still a chance to save our nation.

It cannot be emphasized too strongly or too often that this great nation was founded not by religionists but by Christians, not on religion but on the gospel of Jesus Christ.

—Patrick Henry

I was and always will be a revolutionary communist. I converted to Islam because the Marxist-Leninist revolution today is being achieved through the Koran.

—Venezuelan terrorist Ilich Ramirez Sanchez,
better known as Carlos the Jackal

SOURCES IN ENGLISH

Golitsyn, Anatoliy. 1995. *The Perestroika Deception*. New York: Ed Harle.

Pacepa, Ion, and Ronald J. Rychlak. 2013. *Disinformation*. Washington, DC: WND Books, Inc.

International Committee of the Fourth International website. No author listed. https://www.wsws.org/en/articles/2016/02/29/pers-f29.html [accessed June 25, 2016].

SOURCES IN RUSSIAN

Lecture notes and discussions with students and professors in Moscow, 2012–2013 (the names of the people I talked to cannot be given due to safety and security risks).

Езепчук, Ю.В. 2010. *Одна жизнь на двух континентах*. Москва: Новый Хронограф.

Езепчук, Ю.В. 2015–2016. Personal interviews and discussions.

Appendix 1

• • •

I TOOK THE FOLLOWING PHOTOS while hiking in Golden Gate Canyon State Park, not far from Golden, Colorado, in June of 2013. This structure and stump were located approximately twenty yards or so off the trail and were somewhat hidden from view. I spotted this structure (and later the stump) completely by chance while glancing off to the side of the trail. I recognized these items as being Russian from special training I received while working in law enforcement. The tree stump is used for a game that Russian soldiers play in the forest. The two photos of the structure depict how Russian agents start fires in the United States.

These structures are built near known areas of frequent lightning strikes so that fires will seem to have been caused by lightning. This is precisely where this structure was located—not far from trees that had been hit by lightning in the past. The structure is designed to protect the fire in its early stages from strong winds so that it will eventually burn out of control, especially in dry conditions. I talked with park officers and asked them if they had seen this structure before (or if they had built it for some reason). They said that they were completely unaware and had never seen anything like it before. They immediately dispatched a crew to tear it down. I also asked if they'd had any Russian tourists recently, and they said that the park does have visitors with Eastern European accents from time to time.

Appendix 2: Suggested Further Reading and Viewing

• • •

English for heritage language speakers: http://www.ehlsprogram.org/

K-Love (radio station): http://www.klove.com/

The 1963 goals of communism (the results are visible today): http://www.uhuh.com/nwo/communism/comgoals.htm

Organisation for Islamic Cooperation: http://www.oic-oci.org/oicv3/home/?lan=en

Senate Intelligence Committee Report (proof that the USSR was strengthening, not weakening, during *perestroika*):
https://archive.org/stream/SovietPresenceInTheU.N.Secretariat/Soviet%20Presence%20in%20the%20U.N.%20Secretariat#page/n0/mode/2up

Tudeh Party Iran (the role of communism as the foundation of Islamic revolution beginning in the 1940s demonstrates that communism is alive and well in Iran to this day): http://www.foia.cia.gov/sites/default/files/document_conversions/89801/DOC_0000258385.pdf

Official website of the Commonwealth of Independent States (the site no longer includes an English translation): http://www.cis.minsk.by/

The program of the Communist Party USA: http://cpusa.org/party-program/

International Congress of Industrialists and Entrepreneurs: http://ic-ie.com/en/

The Peoples' Friendship University: http://www.rudn.ru/en_new/

The Shanghai Cooperation Organization (SCO; this site is now available only in Russian and Mandarin Chinese): http://sectsco.org/

About the Author

• • •

Lance Alred has an MA in Russian, a masters of liberal studies in global affairs (with a global-issues concentration) from the University of Denver, a BA in international studies from the University of Denver, an AA degree in general studies with a paralegal emphasis from Arapahoe Community College, and nearly two decades of professional experience in the fields of government, law enforcement, and security.

www.ingramcontent.com/pod-product-compliance
Lightning Source LLC
Chambersburg PA
CBHW072208280526
45788CB00002B/930